A Short History of
American Rowing

Bedlam! The Stroke in a Trireme Catches a Crab!

Even before World War I the annual regattas at Poughkeepsie and New London were attracting spectators by the thousands. Since the latter had to wait a long time between races, the elaborate regatta programs helped to pass the time. This cartoon by Bob Osborn appeared in the 1932 program at New London, together with 150 pages of information about the crews, articles on the theatre, polo and yachting, and tempting advertisements for fur coats, Paris fashions, and a 240 foot Diesel yacht.

A Short History of American Rowing

Thomas C. Mendenhall

CHARLES RIVER BOOKS, BOSTON

Library of Congress Cataloging in Publication Data

Mendenhall, Thomas Corwin.
  A short history of American rowing.

  Bibliography: p.
  1. Rowing—United States—History. I. Title.
GV791.M43   797.1'23   80-22054
ISBN 0-89182-026-4
ISBN 0-89182-028-0 (pbk.)

Published by Charles River Books, Inc.
One Thompson Square, Boston, MA 02129

Copyright © by Charles River Books, Inc.

Contents

ILLUSTRATIONS

To all those who believe
with Ratty that "there is nothing—
absolutely nothing—half so much
worth doing as simply messing about
in boats."

Preface

This book is written out of a conviction that those who enjoy rowing should know its history. Some awareness of how rowing has evolved in this country, some understanding of both the similarities and the contrasts between the development of rowing and other sports should enrich as well as inform. The bond that unites all who have ever rowed, old and young, men and women, novice and elite oarsman, is perhaps unique to rowing and often impossible for non-rowers to appreciate. Technique, training and equipment may have changed over time. Yet some sensations have come to everyone who has ever pulled an oar or scull—frequently for some, occasionally for all—and these provide a congruency of experience, both physical and psychological, which transcends place and time as well as ability: a crisp beginning, a clean release, a space-eating settle after a racing start or the crescendo of a closing sprint.

The race results which make up the second half of this book provide an historical third dimension to some of the fixtures of the rowing year. One of the oldest of sports and the oldest intercollegiate sport in America, rowing again is unique. Its professional period lies far in the past. Today's oarsmen are among the last of the true amateurs in this country. So the catalogue of their ancient rivalries should reinforce the pleasure of the most recent competitors.

For the non-rowing public the book may begin to explain the extraordinary attraction rowing seems to have for all who fall beneath its spell. In the first place there is infinite variety: the loneliness of the single sculler whose fate rests entirely in his own hands; the subtle blending of skill and strength which is required to row a pair or IV without, rowing's equivalent of a string quartet; the powerful unity of an VIII when moving well, perhaps the quintessence of team play. In the jargon of the sociologist, there is no bonding comparable to that of a crew, which is one reason why women are embracing the sport in such enthusiastic numbers. This profound unity carries right into the race itself. In no other sport is a team or crew made to feel so completely on its own: no substitutes, no coaching from the sidelines, no locker-room strategy at half-time. Once the coach has shoved a crew away from the dock, everything is up to them.

Finally, what can be more beautiful than the juncture of body, legs and arms as a skillful sculler or crew fairly lifts the boat along and the water laps gently along the sides of the shell when the crew has heard the "easy all." Few sports can boast such pleasant, varied settings. Over forty years ago an English oarsman caught all this in a poem:

> Seeming monotony! But how it cloaks
> The fineness of art, still mastered, still defeated:
> The balance and the rhythm and the drive
> That weld the crew and make the boat alive
> And keep her running sweetly through the strokes!

This book had its beginnings almost two years ago when the US Olympic Rowing Committee requested a chapter on the history of American rowing. The original venture was abandoned, but it is reappearing in *Rowing Fundamentals—A Manual for Coaches*, which John Ferriss of Cornell is editing. A greatly shortened version of the text will appear in the *Manual*. Meanwhile, John Ferriss has helped especially with the glossary and bibliography of this *Short History*. Peter Raymond, the editor of the *Oarsman*, has been most generous with time, advice and encouragement throughout. Among the officials past and present of the National Association of Amateur Oarsmen, I would thank Evelyn Bergman, Boyce Budd, Jack Franklin, and Hart Perry for their suggestions and assistance. Over the last forty-five years a host of oarsmen, coaches and students of rowing in America and abroad have shared with me their knowledge and love of the sport. Some, like Ed Leader, Tom Bolles and Ky Ebright, three great coaches, are no longer with us. Richard Burnell, who now has a column on England and the international scene in the *Oarsman*, has long been a valued pen-pal. Thirty years of friendship with Joe Burk, perhaps the most imaginative oarsman and coach I have known, have yielded me extra dividends. More recently, Harry Parker, his pupil and friend, has cheerfully fielded my questions. Stan and Lois Pocock generously provided the details of shells and their making.

In preparing the manuscript Pat Waring somehow mastered my handwriting, while Alison Shaw has produced most of the pictures. To my good fortune, Linda Thomas made available the picture for the cover. At Charles River Books, Bruce Comjean has proved cheerfully supportive of a book on rowing. The editor, Dennis Campbell, has attacked with imagination the problems he has encountered. To the above and many more the book owes whatever quality it may have. Its mistakes and excesses must be attributed to my own uncontrolled devotion to the sport.

TCM

A Short History of
American Rowing

Key to the Picture

(1) Button
(2) Deck
(3) Gate
(4) Gunwale
(5) Heel cups
(6) Inboard
(7) Leather
(8) Oarlock
(9) Outboard
(10) Outrigger
(11) Rib
(12) Scull
(13) Slide
(14) Sliding Seat
(15) Stop
(16) Stretcher

Boat	Length	Width at Water Line	Weight
Single	24'–27'	10-1/2"–12"	25–36 lbs.
Double	30'–32'	14"–18"	63–73 lbs.
Quad	39'	20"	130–170 lbs.
Pair without	32'	16"	65–85 lbs.
Pair with	35'	16"	78–100 lbs.
IV without	39'	18"–20"	120–170 lbs.
IV with	42'	20"	85–175 lbs.
VI without	40'–50'	21-1/2"–26"	150 lbs.
VIII	60'	22"–25"	240–300 lbs.

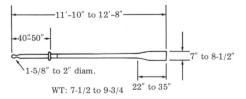

11'-10" to 12'-8"

40"-50"

1-5/8" to 2" diam.

7" to 8-1/2"

22" to 35"

WT: 7-1/2 to 9-3/4

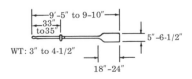

9'-5" to 9-10"

33" to 35"

5"-6-1/2"

WT: 3" to 4-1/2"

18"-24"

Glossary

Back (to) or backwater: to move shell backwards by turning the concave side of the blade toward the bow of the shell and pushing the handle toward the stern.

Blade: the flattened or spoon-shaped outboard end of a scull or sweep. Until late in the 1950s most oar blades were long and thin (needle blades), perhaps 32-inches long and 6 1/2-wide at the tip. Ratzeburg, among its other innovations, then introduced a shorter, wider blade, with the working part of the blade nearer the tip. Since the blade is wider (9-inches) in the middle but tapers towards the tip, it makes possible a more powerful stroke yet gives an easier finish.

Bow: the forward section or nose of the shell.

Bow (man): the oarsman who sits nearest the bow of the shell.

Bowside: all the oarsmen whose oars are in the water on the starboard side of the shell— the left side of the shell as one faces the stern.

Bucket (to): throwing the body forward at the beginning of the recovery, before the arms have been straightened out and before the hands have passed over the knees.

Bucking the oar: to cut short the finish before the hands have come back to the chest.

Button: a wide collar on the leather or plastic sheath of the oar which keeps it from slipping through the oarlock and holds it against the thole pin. A modern button can be adjusted up and down the oar, thus making the leverage easier or harder.

Catch: that part of the stroke when the oar is placed in the water; followed by the pull-through.

Check: an abrupt change in the rate of deceleration caused by pressure on the stretcher without a simultaneous pressure on the pin. Also, a split in the thin wooden skin of the shell.

Clinker: a method of planking in which the lower edge of the plank overlaps the upper edge of the one below it; also called lapstreak. The perfection of a smooth-skinned racing shell a century ago made for a faster boat.

Cockpit: space for one person in a shell, also called stateroom.

Coxswain: steers the shell, usually from a seat in the stern, though in a modern Pair, or IV with, the coxswain sometimes is lying down in the bow to reduce air resistance and spread the weight over more of the boat.

Crab: occurs when an oarsman finds it difficult or impossible to get the oar out of the water at the end of the pull-through. He may have gone too deep or become hung up on a wave or another's puddle.

Deck: the areas of a shell at the bow and stern which are covered with varnished cloth or more recently with a thin plastic material.

Double: a sculling boat for two rowers.

Drive: the part of the stroke cycle between the catch and the release; also called the pull-through.

Easy all: the command to stop rowing and let the oars rest flat on the water. The same as "weigh enough" or "weigh all."

Eight or VIII: a sweep boat with rowers and a coxswain.

Endurance Training: exercises designed to improve the crew's ability to continue without stopping, usually of medium intensity for long periods of time.

Feather: to turn the blade over parallel to the surface of the water at the end of the pull-through and the start of the recovery in order to lessen the wind resistance of the blade and facilitate the release.

FISA: *the Fédération internationale des sociétès d'aviron*, the international governing body of rowing, a federation of national organizations formed in 1892.

Fin: a small flat piece of metal or wood attached perpendicular to the bottom of the shell to help keep the shell on a true course.

Finish: that part of the pull-through or stroke just before the oar is taken from the water.

Fixed pin: a form of oarlock in which the oar slides between two vertical wooden pins which do not move.

Four or IV: a sweep boat for four rowers, either with or without a coxswain.

Gate: a bar across the oarlock to retain the oar.

German rig: the normal rig of a shell has the oars alternated from bow to stern. The boat is not truly balanced, for the bowside oarsmen are two feet nearer the bow than stroke side. To compensate for this Karl Adam put two rowers (four and five) on the same side, with the others alternating as before.

Gunwale: the horizontal strips of wood running the whole length of the shell on both sides, to which the ribs, knees and skin are attached.

Handle: the part of the oar which is grasped by the oarsman.

Heel cups: metal or plastic cups for supporting the heels on the stretchers.

Henley Distance: one and five sixteenth miles; taken from the Henley-on-Thames course. This is a competitive distance often rowed by crews at English, American and Canadian Henley Regattas. Increasingly it is being replaced by the Olympic distance (2000 meters).

Hold all: the command given by the coxswain to have the oarsmen place their blades horizontally in the water to stop the shell quickly.

Interval training: a method which originated with Swedish long distance runners and seeks to develop stamina and thus speed over a certain distance. Speed-play was adapted for rowing by Karl Adam at Ratzeburg. In preparing for a 2000 meter race, a crew will row four or more stretches of 400 to 600 meters in order to determine and learn the best speed for that crew at that point in its training.

Italian rig: a more extensive, uneven alteration of the normal rig than the German, with all but stroke and bow rowing in pairs on alternate sides.

Inside Hand: the rowers hand nearest the oarlock.

Keel: the long wood member running the length of the boat along the centerline of the shell, to which all other parts are attached.

Keelson: a support member between the keel and the seat braces.

Knee: the wooden support inside a shell connecting keel, gunwale, washboard and outrigger.

Knifing in: the fault often caused by under-squaring the blade at the catch so that the oar goes too deep when power is applied; also may result in a crab.

Lapstreak: see clinker.

Layback: the amount of backward lean of the oarsman's body toward the bow at the finish of the release.

Leather: the leather or plastic sheath around the oar to keep the rowlock from wearing out the oar; also known as sleeve.

Length in the Water: the arc in the water through which the blade moves during the drive. It can vary with the rower's reach, the amount of slide used, the layback, the length of the oar and the ratio of inboard to outboard.

Loom: the shaft or part of the oar between the blade and the handle.

NAAO: formed in 1872, the National Association of Amateur Oarsmen is the governing organization of amateur rowing in the United States.

Oar (sweep): a first and second-class lever approximately twelve-feet long, weighing six pounds or more, by which the oarsman pulls against the oarlock to move the boat through the water. The distance between the far end of the handle and the face of the button touching the oarlock is called the inboard of the oar or scull. The part remaining, out to the tip of the blade, is called the outboard.

Oarlock: a U-shaped swivel of cast metal or plastic which holds the oar in the outrigger. The oarlock is mounted on the sill and rotates around a vertical thole pin, with a gate at the top to secure the oar.

Outrigger or Rigger: a metal framework of two or three stays to support the oarlock which is placed about 30-inches out from the center of the shell and attached by bolts to two or three knees of the shell.

Outside Hand: the rower's hand furthest away from the oarlock.

Port: the left side of the shell as one faces the bow.

Puddles: whirls left in the water from the blade slipping as the rower pulls.

Racing Start: the first 20 to 40 strokes of a race which are usually quicker than those used throughout the race. The first few strokes of the start are usually shorter in order to get the shell moving.

Rating: rate of striking, or cadence, the number of strokes per minute that a crew is rowing.

Recovery: the part of the stroke cycle between the release and the catch in which the oar is made ready for the catch and the seat returned to the stern end of the slide.

Release: the part of the stroke cycle when the oar is taken from the water and feathered.

Ribs: small pieces of wood which support the hull by fitting inside the shell between the keel and gunwale.

Rig: arrangement of riggers (and hence oars and rowers) in a shell: standard, German, or Italian.

Rhythm: for any one crew the proportion of time occupied on the recovery to the time taken on the pull through; effective rhythm will help produce the best results for the power expended.

Rudder: the steering device on the stern of the shell or under the shell (a fin rudder). Rudder lines connect the rudder through pulleys either to the coxswain or in a Pair, IV without or VI without, to the stretcher of the oarsman who is steering.

Run: of a shell, the distance it travels during one stroke. In the water, run is shown by the distance between successive puddles from the same oar and is a good guide to the pace of a shell.

Sculls: the shorter oars (9-foot 6-inches to 10-feet in length) used in pairs for Singles, Doubles, or Quads.

Single: a sculling boat for one person.

Slide: a seat which moves on wheels up and down two parallel runners 27 to 32-inches long. There are stops at the front (stern) and back (bow) of the tracks to prevent the seat from sliding off. Normally a crew would slide up to its work (i.e. the middle of the holes in the seat being even with the rowing pin when the seat is at the stern end of the tracks), but it can be stopped either through or behind its work.

Spacing: the distance between successive sets of puddles. Spacing varies with a crew's ability and especially with the rating. It is often measured and compared by relating the sternpost to the next set of puddles.

Speed training: exercises designed to improve the speed of a crew, always done in the interval form.

Splash Guard: canvas strips stretched along the outriggers next to the gunwales, in order to prevent water from slopping into the shell in very rough weather.

Starboard: the right side of the boat as one faces the bow.

Standard rig: uniform alternation of riggers (and hence oars and rowers) in a shell.

Stretcher: the oarsman's feet are fixed on the stretcher which consists of two inclined footrests or clogs or light shoes mounted on a frame attached to the top to the inside of the gunwale and at the bottom to the keel. Laces or straps hold the feet on the footrest. The whole stretcher is movable backwards and forwards and fixed with thumb screws to allow oarsmen of different leg lengths to use as much slide as possible.

Stroke: the rower nearest the stern who sets the rhythm and cadence for a crew. Also the complete cycle of the rowing motion consisting of catch, pull through (drive), finish, release and feather and recovery.

Swing: a harmony of movement between men and boat.

Thwart: fixed-seat in a small boat.

Training: a planned program of gradually increasing physical load designed to strengthen qualities valuable to rowing; see endurance, speed, interval.

Washing Out: occurs when the blade comes out of the water during the drive before the finish, with a consequent loss of power.

The Beginnings

The origins of boatracing lie far back in human history. Indeed, if one assumes that competition also lies deep in the human psyche, primitive man must early on have raced to see who could run the fastest, had the fastest horse or the fastest boat. As soon as the second reed-boat or dugout canoe was built, the first one must have been challenged to a race across the river or around the point. Clearly the paddle was the first way to propel a boat. But sometime after 1000 B.C. an oar working against a fulcrum was found to be appreciably more effective mechanically (by about fifty per cent) than a paddle. Although fishermen are still occasionally seen sculling while facing the bow, the human body, whether sitting or standing, can lever a boat through the water more efficiently when facing the stern. Thus the old chestnut of the uninitiated about the stupid oarsman who can't even see where he is going must be one of the oldest of jokes.

Today competitive rowing is essentially a leisure-time activity. This is not to deny that it is hard work, ranking indeed with the most energy-demanding of sports, but rather to state that now there are no professionals, except coaches, who make their living out of rowing. This has not always been the case. Before the appearance of organized sports there were professional watermen who supported themselves with the oar. Boats racing grew out of boats working. In 1716 in England it was his gratitude for the Thames watermen who taxied him to work that led **Thomas Doggett**, the actor, to endow annual races for apprentice watermen; the winner received an orange coat and a silver badge engraved with the word *Liberty*. Similarly, less than a half-

5

century later it was the races between the watermen in New York harbor which launched boat racing in this country. Originally **Doggett's Coat and Badge** was contested in heavy boats capable of carrying a passenger; today the young watermen race over the five miles from London Bridge to Chelsea in light singles. The New York watermen first raced at the urging of their passengers, usually in fours to cope with the more exposed reaches of the harbor, in heavy but fine-lined lap-streak boats which took their name from the Whitehall landing at the foot of the Battery.

In May 1843, a Yale junior brought a secondhand Whitehall boat, costing $29.50 with oars, back to New Haven to form the first boatclub at Yale College. Scratch races and informal tests of skill and strength inevitably followed, thus introducing intramural boatracing to American colleges. Almost ten years before, in 1834, the organization of the **Castle Garden Amateur Boat Club Association** with nine member clubs marked the beginning of club rowing in New York harbor. Rival groups soon appeared along the Hudson. Rowing for racing as well as recreation spread rapidly over the country into the harbors, up the rivers, even following the Gold Rush into San Francisco. The **Detroit Boat Club,** founded in 1839, has the honor of being the oldest club in this country still active in the sport. The **Schuylkill Navy,** first organized in 1858, was to give the Philadelphia clubs a structure and a permanent role in American rowing.

Meanwhile, some of the professional watermen were finding it possible to make a living by racing for money. By the Civil War the **Biglin Brothers,** the **Wards,** and **James Hamill** of Pittsburgh were gaining national reputations, racing for anything from $50 to $3000 in fours, pairs, doubles or singles, and providing the public with their first sporting heroes, the press with constant copy, and **Thomas Eakins,** the painter, with some of his best models. In those early years racing remained informal, infrequent and unselective with undergraduates or amateurs rowing against professionals in the Boston City, Castle Garden or Newburgh regattas—and taking the purse or prize money if they were skillful enough to win.

That sports are man-made or socially-conditioned (to quote a sociological truism) is proved by the way they burst into being in the fifteen years after the Civil War. Thanks to continued immigrations and the transportation revolution, America progressively by regions was losing its frontier. As the country filled up, what could replace this elbow room, provide the safety valve for the now crowded townsman and occupy the energies of what had always been a nation of activists? Sports and outdoor pastimes, more than any other single thing, were to fill the gap. Throughout the country, boatracing was among the leaders in this procession, thanks to the professional scullers, the amateur members of the rowing clubs and college students. Though today crew ranks low as a spectator sport, a century ago it acted as the herald of all the mass excitement to come. In the late fifties and sixties

The Biglen Brothers Turning the Stake

The burst of sporting activity in late 19th century America fortunately attracted the interest of one of the country's greatest painters. A sculler himself, the Philadelphia artist Thomas Eakins (1844–1916) was particularly attracted to the human body in action. Thus, the two professional scullers had to row briefly against each other as they raced around the turning stake.

of the nineteenth-century there were as many as ten or a dozen regattas per year; for 1867 some forty-eight different match races and regattas are listed; the figure reached sixty-five for 1869, and over one-hundred-fifty for 1872; everywhere from Savannah to Sacramento, from Maine to Milwaukee, for anything from $500 to Kyle's Gold Badge or the weighty honor of pulling two passengers thirty-three miles around Manhattan Island in five and a half hours.

The Equipment Available

Before attempting even the briefest history of a century of American rowing, some account must be given of what equipment was available at different times (what one rows with). Technology must come first because every major change in equipment has eventually produced or even required a rethinking of technique and training.

Racing could take place either in sculling boats or in rowing boats. A **sculling boat** is either a single, a double (two scullers) or a quad (four scullers) and usually does not carry a coxswain. Each person holds a scull in each hand. In a **rowing boat** each person holds one sweep oar with both hands. Sweep rowing may involve eight, six, four or two persons and a coxswain; a VI, IV, or pair can be raced with or without a cox. Of necessity a scull (9 feet or more) is shorter and lighter than a sweep which may be 12 feet or longer.

The single scull soon came to represent the original, basic racing boat. Critical improvements or changes usually appeared there first, and other combinations (double sculls, pairs, IVs, VIs and VIIIs) appeared and disappeared unpredictably. During most of the nineteenth-century England was the laboratory for boatbuilding, with her oarsmen experimenting and writing about the art and her builders perfecting most of the changes in boats and oars. By 1811 the Eton boys were racing regularly in VIIIs with cox; the Oxford colleges followed suit in 1815; and in 1829 the first Boat Race between Oxford and Cambridge was rowed over the two and a quarter miles from Hambledon Lock up to Henley Bridge, not for a side bet of £ 500 as the sporting press reported, but only "as a trial of strength and skill" in the reassuring phrase of one of the oarsmen to his anxious mother. One of the original college VIIIs, the Oxford boat of 1829 has been miraculously preserved and can be seen today in the South Kensington Science Museum. Clinker-built and inrigged with thole pins, she 45 feet 4 inches overall with only 28 inches of stateroom for each oarsman, compared with over 50 inches needed today with sliding seats. Balanced on a 7 inch thwart, the oarsmen rowed with enormous sweeps which varied in length from 13 feet 6 inches to 14 feet 6 inches to fit the beam which varied from bow (3 feet 9 inches) to stroke (3 feet 11 inches). The 1829 boat weighed 600 pounds, perhaps two and a half times as much as a modern light VIII, which yielded a very short run between strokes and required a high rate of striking.

About fifty years and three major improvements lay between the 1829 boat and the modern VIII. The first of these improvements in time was the

The Oxford shell of 1829, on the left, shows the narrow seat or thwart and the wooden thole pin fixed on the gunwale. The shell of a century later still has wooden thole pins on the outriggers instead of swivels.

development of **the iron outrigger** by the Clasper family of watermen and professional scullers. Originally used in sculling boats and IVs, it was first used by Oxford and Cambridge in the 1846 Boat Race. The outrigger simplified the equation between beam and leverage and resulted in a much longer and narrower VIII, up to 66 feet in length with a beam of less than 2 feet. The second great improvement came in the next decade with **the keelless boat,** first used by VIIIs in the 1857 Boat Race. Without an exterior keel and with a smooth skin, such a hull further cut down both the weight and wetted surface, while opening up the possibility of endless experimenting with the taper and length.

Although greased pants on a wider thwart had occasionally been tried, it was an American sculler who came upon the third improvement—**the sliding seat.** Actually, he was trying to solve a problem arising out of rigger-spread where the ideal of a good beginning seemed attainable only with a moving oarlock. That proved impossible, but a moving seat was first tried in a light VI in a Hudson River regatta in 1870; Yale tried the moving seat the same year, followed by Harvard in 1872. The sliding seat was first truly appreciated in England as potentially the most important technical innovation since the introduction of the outrigger. With the help of the sliding seat, two advantages quickly became apparent: first, the oarsman was able to increase the length of his stroke, i.e. the time his oar was covered and thus moving the boat; and second, by comparison with fixed-seat rowing, where the stroke was very largely taken by the back and arms, the sliding seat made it possible to harness much more of the oarsman's legs into the stroke.

Although it was almost universally adopted immediately in both America and England, the true potential of the sliding seat would only slowly be appreciated. At first, as an almost vestigial remnant of the fixed seat, all crews were stopped back of their work by 4 or 5 inches. It was 1885 before truly long slides were generally used. The first primitive sliding seats—leather-covered 10 inch squares of wood with grooves on the side which moved fore and aft on two brass rods—were also likely to break down. Finally, the best use of this new improvement was to prove most elusive stylistically. Some would be too concerned to preserve the handsome, long, back swing of fixed-seat rowing; others would so glory in the newfound possibilities of leg-drive that the stroke would degenerate into nothing more than a bum-shove. The sliding seat made possible a much greater use of the legs in the stroke. As a result, how most effectively to combine back, legs and arms would henceforth become the central problem in the formulation of any rowing style.

Sometime in the 1870s, **the swivel oarlock** was invented as an alternative to the older system of a vertical rowing thole (the fixed pin) and a stopping thole. In America oarsmen quickly shifted to the swivel, primarily because the latter is an easier rig to row on. In England the fixed pin lasted much longer since it was considered to be more efficient at both the beginning and the end of the stroke. In both countries the swivel became universal for sculling boats.

In England the **VIII** had early on become **the boat** for intercollegiate racing, although races for small boats (singles, pairs and IVs) had been a regular part of the intramural program at Oxford and Cambridge since the 1840s, as well as a prominent feature of the Henley Regatta since the middle of the century. In America, however, by the late 1850s both Harvard and Yale had become so wedded to the light VI (without cox) for some peculiar reason that when the rowing mania hit the other colleges they all started in VIs. Since their 1859 race, the Harvard and Yale shells were rigged so that Bow could steer with a primitive form of wire attached to his stretcher and running back to the yoke in the rudder such as is now used on a light IV or light pair. In a VI the crew's names still harked back to the original ship's boat: Bow, port Bow, starboard Waist, port Waist, starboard Stroke and Stroke! Bow steering was not adopted in England until ten years later, and eventually the three races for IVs at Henley became limited to light IVs.

Why American collegians stuck so long to the light VI remains something of a mystery. While either a IV or a VI without cox was obviously faster than a IV with, the lack of a coxswain helped produce the endless fouls, accidents and recriminations that plagued the regattas of the short-lived **Rowing Association of American Colleges** in the 1870s. Earlier races were a mile

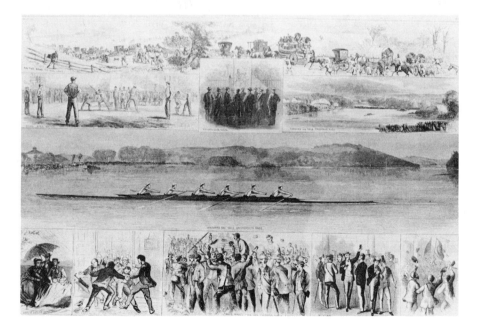

A college regatta such as the Harvard-Yale race of 1867 at Worcester (above) soon became a public occasion, accompanied by a baseball game and the presence of gamblers.

and a half each way around a stake, which could give the spectators a glimpse of both start and finish. The first Association race in 1871 was a three-mile straightaway, which at least eliminated the chaos around the turning stake. Two years later the use of stake-boats "in the English way" at the start proved fairer and less risky. But the mind boggles at the inevitable confusion of eleven VIs, without benefit of coxswain or lane markers, racing down the Connecticut for three miles, especially since the referee's steamlaunch was struggling along a good half-mile behind the crews. Both Harvard and Yale were coming to see the advantage of the VIII (with cox, of course) but the other colleges kept voting down the suggestion, primarily because in a student body of less than two hundred, eight oarsmen were just that much less available than six. By 1876 the British model of the Oxford and Cambridge race and continuing dissatisfaction with the uncertainties of straight VIs racing abreast for three miles led Yale to withdraw from the Association and to challenge Harvard to the first intercollegiate four mile race for VIIIs in America.

While the 1876 race was the seventeenth time the two colleges had raced each other since 1852, their race that June actually began a new chapter in American rowing. Within twenty years the VIII would become the popular combination among college oarsmen, to the eventual exclusion of small boats. As a result, the latter were left until quite recently to the rowing clubs, while the professionals never took up VIIIs. Unfortunately, these contrasts in rig worked to separate rather than unite the rowing interests in this country.

Meanwhile, some critical technical developments still lay ahead: lighter, adjustable riggers, with the elimination of the lower brace which made the going so wet in rough water; lighter boats and oars; the eventual development of adjustable buttons which allowed the leverage to be changed to suit the conditions; the interesting possibilities of plywood and fiber glass, some of which the paper boats made popular from 1875 to 1895 would realize. The major achievements in boatbuilding technology, while realized a good century ago, left the fundamental problems more distinct, but did not bring their resolution any closer. "Given the total weight to be carried, is there any relation between length and speed? Or between beam and speed? What is the right curve for the master section?" These are only some of the imponderables to be resolved every time a new shell is designed or built.

The Rise and Fall
of the
Professional Oarsmen

While it was the professionals, especially the scullers, who inaugurated competitive rowing in this country, by 1900 they had virtually disappeared. Their influence as well as their colorful careers entitle them to a place in any rowing history. The professional IVs of the 1860s gave way to the amateur IVs, but more especially to the enormous popularity of professional sculling over the next twenty years. Rowing and sailing were the only sports featured in the Philadelphia Centennial Exposition of 1876. There the professional sculling reflected the enormous and very international nature of the sport. Beside the best Americans the entries included Higgins of London and three Canadians. One of them, the twenty-one year old **Edward Hanlan** or Toronto, was the unexpected victor, thus beginning a career which would take him to England, all over the United States, including the Pacific coast, and even Australia on innumerable exhibitions and races as he alternately defended or pursued the elusive title of World's Champion. In 1884 he finally lost the title in England to William Beach, an Australian, but he was racing as late as 1897.

Perhaps Hanlan's greatest American rival was **Charles Courtney** who had won the amateur sculling competition at the Centennial Regatta. Older and heavier than Hanlan and victor in over eighty-eight races, Courtney turned professional in 1877. Amid the usual fanfare in the press and the frantic hedging among the gamblers, three races between the two were arranged. The first—over five miles with one turn at Lachine, Canada—resulted in a Hanlan victory by little more than a length, and under sufficiently suspicious circum-

13

With its supreme confidence in material progress, the 19th century invented the
International Exhibition. In 1876 Philadelphia was the obvious place and time for
America's first one. Only two sports were featured—sailing and rowing. The race
for International Amateur IVs (over a mile and half straightaway) included a dozen
American clubs, crews from Columbia and Yale, and three crews from aborad. In
one of the semifinals, Yale (with Bob Cook steering from bow) lost to the London
Rowing Club IV by five feet in the best time of the regatta (8:51.2).

stances to generate great interest in a return match. This was to take place on
Lake Chautauqua in October, 1879. Hop Bitters, "The Invalid's Friend and
Hope," was already suspect as a patent medicine when its promoter sought
to increase sales by signing on the two professional scullers to a five-mile race
for $6,000. As the great day approached, commercialism and speculation
reached a fever pitch, to climax on the morning of the race when Courntey's
shell was found sawed in half. His refusal to race in a borrowed boat left him
open to charges of collusion with one part of the gambling fraternity. Hanlan
rowed over alone, only to have the wily promoter sequester the purse on the
grounds of no race. This scandal did much to darken the good name of professional sculling, which Courtney did nothing to clear by dropping out of
their third and last race the next year. The day was hot, but Hanlan was far
ahead when Courtney stopped at the end of two miles.

Since living on the water or working on the waterfront provided the ob-
vious first step to a rowing career, such ports as Halifax, New York, Portland
(Maine) and especially Boston became the centers for professional scullers.
Hanlan was raised on an island, now Hanlan Island, in Toronto harbor.
Courtney grew up on Lake Cayuga. In Cambridge **George Faulkner**, a suc-

Never defeated as an amateur sculler, Charles Courtney won 88 races. After a more controversial career as a professional (39 victories and 7 defeats), he retired in 1885 to coach Cornell. There for 33 years as the first full-time professional coach, he achieved the remarkable record of more than 100 victories in 146 races. This picture from the *New York Clipper*, a typical "sporting and theatrical" weekly, shows how rowing was sharing in America's search for leisure time activity.

"THE UNITED STATES A SPORTING COUNTRY."
CHORUS OF GRADUATES.—"What's the use of going through col ye, anyhow? It's muscle, and not brains, that wins all the prizes."

Although it could not foresee the degree to which colleges would become the training ground for professional sports, this 1881 cartoon is prophetic of the material success surrounding professional athletes a century later. For better or worse, the professional oarsman was destined to disappear.

cessful sculler and one of Harvard's first coaches (1885), supervised the unloading of coal barges on the Charles. The stakes for which the scullers raced varied from $25 for the beginners in heavy work boats to the $5,000 or more that was needed to get a fine boat race with Hanlan who won almost $12,000 in 1879. If one was really sure of a victory, side bets could increase the take. In addition, there were always exhibitions, the opportunity perhaps to coach a rowing club for the summer, and even the raffle of the shell after the race. A man might retire to the safer profession of a boat-builder, like Michael Davis of Portland who held over a dozen patents on swivels, sliding seats and leg-of-mutton oars.

Already a century ago sports were beginning to fulfill in a timely fashion a timeless need for public entertainment for the urban masses. Professional sculling was among the first to appear. Although hardly the ideal spectator sport, it was able to provide the sporting press with enough gossip, rumor and human interest to make the scullers the folk heroes of the day. The races themselves were always late and usually dull, since most spectators could only see the start and the finish which often became a procession. But a regatta was an outing, an event with crowds, food, drink, gamblers and plenty of excitement besides the races.

After Portland's **Michael Davis** beat Boston's **George Faulkner** before 30,000 people on the Charles in June 1877, **Patsy Reagan** was chosen to match Davis' challenge to any Boston sculler to a four-mile race for $1,000 a side. Each sculler or his backers put up $1,000 in this winner take all event. Originally planned for a Saturday on the Charles, the race was moved to Silver Lake twenty miles south of Boston on an October Tuesday in 1878, under pressure from the Old Colony Railroad which was trying to make the lake popular—and profitable—as a resort. Despite the loss of a day's pay, over 1000 fans crowded into the twenty-two cars of the excursion train. The race for the championship of New England became of great interest to the betting fraternity, with frantic betting as the odds moved suspiciously from 3 to 1 for Reagan to 4 to 1 against him. Davis won by nine lengths in record time. Amid cries of "foul" and "all bets off," Regan, his disconsolate supporters and the excursion train started back for Boston, only to smash into a freight train at Wollaston, injuring 190 people and killing 19, including Patsy Reagan himself. Boston was desolated. In the words of Sylvester Gookin, who has lovingly chronicled this unhappy saga: "While only 1,500 people took a workaday Tuesday off to see Reagan row what turned out to be his last race, there were nearly 6,000 who took off a workaday Friday to bid him farewell."

Whether as games or as exercise, sports have always contributed to the individual participant, to his pleasure, to his good health and even to his character. But early on in this country sports acquired an obligation to provide public entertainment. As for professional sports, entertaining the public was indeed their only justification. In addition to a general agreement on a minimum of rules (how two scullers, for instance, should turn around a single stake), some kind of sponsorhsip became all-important for the survival of a sport. As a pioneer, professional sculling found two kinds of sponsors available—commercial interests and the gamblers. Unfortunately, the combined influence of these two groups contributed to the early demise of professional sculling and rowing as a sport. While rowing could not offer business very much of the direct profit that Remington Rifles, Goodyear's Rubber Fishing Outfit or Imperial Croquet or Lawn Pool represented, at its height professional sculling appealed to the promotional side of a product like Hop Bitters. The famous Chautauqua fiasco, however, showed how difficult it was to keep the self-serving gamblers from ruining the sport. Of course, the gamblers first helped to stimulate public interest by setting the odds. But for the professional gambler the odds are a tempting way to the true killing. If they can somehow be manipulated rather than simply estimated, the slaughter of the innocents becomes truly monumental. Soon in professional sculling, as was to happen later in baseball and other sports, the combination of commercialism, publicity and the determination of some gamblers to fix the outcome, placed the races and even the scullers themselves under increasing temptation, pressure and suspicion. Was it all fair and square or were the races somehow, sometimes rigged?

Despite their virtual disappearance by 1900 the professional scullers left a most important legacy. Rowing lightly by today's figures (most of them under 160 pounds) and racing usually for five miles around a stake, they

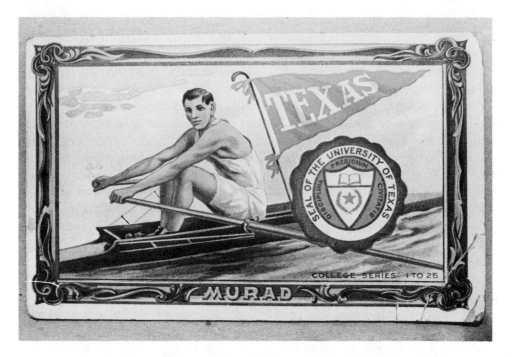

Would rowing help sell cigarettes? In 1911 one company thought so. Fifteen coupons taken from Murad Cigarettes would get you a picture of one of the 25 scullers in the College Series. Less than a third of the colleges in the Series actually had crew, but that did not matter to Murad.

proved the old truism that mileage makes champions and physical condition is vital. Many of them were sons of Irish immigrants for whom sport was a welcome avenue of upward mobility. Even though formal racing between amateurs or college students and the professional disappeared with the scandals of the 1870s, informal brushes while practicing on the Charles, the Hudson or the Schuylkill helped sport to acquire one of its most valuable social functions in a democracy.

Perhaps the most important part of the professional scullers' legacy lay in their emphasis on perfection of watermanship through the use of small boats. A single, where the variables are reduced to the boat, the rig, the conditions and the individual oarsman, has always offered the clearest path to effective, powerful and successful rowing. Almost seventy years ago the achievement of the professional sculler was described as follows:

It takes years of patient study and hard work and blade action to attain firm blade "footing" in the water; and until this is secured, no amount of sheer strength will command good speed.

Obviously sweep rowing differs significantly from sculling and some scullers have depended too much on a strong back and arms, a high rating, and a rush at the finish; but the good sculler must acquire an easy combination of body, slide and arms, a smooth horizontal movement of blades and boat through the water, and a quick, neat steady recovery. In the history of American rowing the rise and fall of this sculling tradition correlates significantly with the popularity as well as the good health of the sport.

Although in the early 1870s both club and college rowing chose to disassociate themselves formally from the professionals and their "dirty tricks," it was not very realistic for American rowing to proscribe professional watermen in favor of amateur coaches at that moment and in this country. The example of England was very appealing but not too relevant. There in a country of modest size with a well-established sporting tradition such a group had already emerged: amateurs of independent means in sufficient numbers to provide coaches and expertise for both universities and clubs. Indeed, the unpaid amateur coach became the rule in England from that day to this. Little wonder that American rowing, already looking to England for so much in the way of technique and training, should seek to emulate this ideal of the gentleman-amateur coach. Over the years before World War I many of the great English names in this tradition would be lured over to this country as consultants and even coaches. The end of such visitors came in 1921 with the dramatic departure of **Guy Nickalls** from Yale as a result of his characterizing the Varsity as "gutless."

Meanwhile, a steady effort had been made to find such amateur coaches of independent means in this country. If anywhere they were to be found among the rowing alumni. Early on these individuals had become very active in college rowing, thereby filling the void left by the reluctance of college faculties and administrations to assume any responsibility either for money or for athletic policy. But the social and economic ethos of late nineteenth-century America worked against the emergence of such individuals in any numbers, with sufficient means, leisure and skill. **Bob Cook** at Yale was the great exception. He towered over Yale rowing from 1872 to 1896 with fourteen out of nineteen victories. His personality could be felt all the way from Philadelphia where he managed a newspaper and somehow found the time for brief visits to New Haven and New London. No other college could produce an amateur-alumnus coach with anything like his record of success.

It was inevitable from 1880s on that the professional scullers would creep back into the picture as coaches, with some of their tricks and more secretiveness about their crews and their progress than was good for the sport. Yet their knowledge and experience was invaluable. **Faulkner** and **James Wray** (1905-15) at Harvard, **Michael Davis** and **John Kennedy** (1906-11) at Yale, **Jim Ten Eyck** at Syracuse (1903-38) and **Ellis Ward** at Pennsylvania were some of the great names, but **Pop Courtney** at Cornell from 1885 to

1919 was perhaps the most famous and successful. Of some 146 Cornell crews which he coached, 101 of them were winners. In twenty-four Poughkeepsie races, his Cornell Varsities finished first fourteen times and were never worse than third. His great rival, Ned Hanlan, coached Columbia for a few years at the very end of his life. Except for one epic race in 1901 when Columbia drove Cornell to a course record, his results were not distinguished, thus reaffirming the truism that great performers do not necessarily make great teachers.

A less desirable contribution of the professionals to American rowing was their suspected willingness to resort to sharp tricks, often under pressure from their backers. This led to an unnecessary secretiveness in their coaching, concerning both their style or stroke and the performance of a particular crew. This became most noticeable when one of them would take a crew to England and Henley where the proximity of the tow path and the coach on a horse or bicycle had long resulted in an easy exchange of information and expertise. In 1901, for instance, Ellis Ward whispered to his crew through a megaphone lest, as he said later, some spy might reveal the secrets of the "Pennsylvania stroke" to their rivals.

The very fact that the professionals appeared early and disappeared soon was to have several interesting effects on American rowing. The abuses that overtook and eventually overpowered professional rowing worked to split them apart from both the clubs and the college oarsmen. In 1872 the original charter of the National Association of Amateur Oarsmen carefully excluded from the amateur ranks any oarsman who obtained any kind of "pecuniary" benefit from rowing. The next year the Rowing Association of American Colleges agreed not to use professional trainers after that year's regatta. Because in fact proper amateur coaches did not appear in any number, as has already been explained, the professional scullers soon emerged to coach, often almost surreptitiously as riggers or trainers. This worked to prevent the development of the coaching profession until World War I and after. In the longer run the fate of the professional sculler was one of the reasons why rowing's history was to prove quite different from that of the other sports in this country. Sooner or later most sports or games, especially as they became part of the entertainment business, have progressed from a broad base of people who play for fun and exercise to the development of a hierarchy by ability up to the paid professional at the top. Baseball, football, basketball, or ice hockey all illustrate this sequence. Admittedly these late-comers had not only greater appeal for spectators but could also be staged to yield more income at the gate. Yet the early rise and fall of professional oarsmen, for whatever combination of reasons, left rowing without the more normal structure and destined to have a rather different evolution than other sports, freer from commercial pressures and able to champion and maintain a unique version of the amateur athlete.

Club Rowing
and the Amateur

The two most active periods in American rowing have occurred almost a century apart. Ushered in by the professional scullers, the decade of the 1870s saw rowing more widely enjoyed than at any time from then until today and more popular than ever before or since. The popularity was an historical accident. More leisure, greater affluence and expanding cities combined to provide both participants and spectators. Rowing, like horse-racing, was on hand to meet the needs of both. The railroad and the telegraph worked to make this activity regional and even national, bringing competitors and crowds together, broadcasting the results, and producing a half-dozen sporting weeklies to stimulate the rivalry and delight the fans. Soon rowing would be overtaken and passed by baseball, running and bicycling, as well as by such less strenuous alternatives as tennis or croquet. In 1873, as the NAAO was just being formed, the Aquatics Editor of *Turf, Field and Farm* published the first *Boating Almanac* and *Boat Club Directory*. While admitting that some clubs were not as active as others, he listed 289 organized boat clubs in twenty-five states. New York led the list with seventy-four; but Georgia with twelve, Michigan with fourteen, Iowa's five and California's fourteen showed how boating had swept the country. Of the 159 races or regattas listed for the year, fifteen were scheduled for the Fourth of July. Some of these clubs had been boating for pleasure, if not racing, for over thirty years; others, like the Schuylkill Navy, had developed regional associations. Originally the racing was in small boats (singles, doubles sculls, pairs, light IVs and even light VIs), usually for a mile and a half with one turn. With the first appearance of VIIIs in club racing in 1880 the turn had to be eliminated. The first regattas were open to professionals as well as amateurs, and the amateurs had no hesitation about accepting a purse if they won.

By 1872 interest in racing was so great that heats were first required to cope with the large number of entries at the Schylkill Navy's regatta. At this point the questionable station of some of the entrants led to the definition of an amateur and the organization of the NAAO. Today, as in all sports, the distinction between an amateur and a professional is under challenge, review and revison. And historically the distinction has often had a determining influence on the development of the sport. So some definitions and a bit of history are in order.

Despite their obvious Latin roots, the meanings which have produced so much argument first appeared in the nineteenth-century. The amateur cultivated any activity, especially a sport, as a pastime in contrast to the professional who pursued the same activity to earn his living. Both terms might be used disparagingly: the amateur was sometimes seen as the dabbler or dilettante; to be labeled a professional politician was rarely a compliment; and the professional athlete was often dismissed as vulgar or lower-class as compared with the gentleman amateur. But the two could never remain long apart in any sport. More intense practice and greater technical skill usually made the professional in demand as a teacher. The natural urge either to test oneself against the best or to discover who was better inevitably brought amateur and professional together, at least into informal competition. Yet by 1872 the lovers of rowing for its own sake—the amateurs—had become sufficiently suspicious of those who were making rowing a business (not so much of their skill as of their tricks and their gambler associates) to insist on distinguishing between them. The first American definition of an amateur spells out the difference:

> One who does not enter into an open competition; or for either stake, public or admission money or entrance fee; or compete with or against a professional for any prize; who has never taught, pursued, or assisted in the pursuit of athletic exercises as a means of livelihood; whose membership of any rowing or any other athletic club was not brought about, or does not continue, because of any mutual agreement or understanding, expressed or implied, whereby his becoming or continuing a member of such club would be of any pecuniary benefit to him whatever, direct or indirect; who has never been employed in any occupation involving any use of the oar or paddle; who rows for pleasure or recreation only, and during his leisure hours; who does not abandon or neglect his usual business or occupation for the purpose of training, and who shall otherwise conform to the rules and regulations of this association.

Over the next decade two parts of this very American definition would be strengthened. On the one hand, such suspicious incidents as the Hop Bitters Race of 1879 increased the professionals' reputation for shady tricks while confirming the amateurs' suspicions. Almost fifty years later the committee of Yale oarsmen, which was eventually to bring Ed Leader to New Haven, decided not to consider a professional sculler of great distinction as a candidate because he might teach the young men such "tricks." On the other hand, the American amateur was not seen as a gentleman whose independent income gave him the leisure to row for pleasure, but rather as a working man whose job or business would effectively prevent him from training as regularly or extensively as a professional. In America the Calvinist work ethic had somehow to come to terms with a growing national interest in leisure and play.

A few years later, in 1878, the English defined an amateur oarsman in very much the same fashion, but with one significant addition: he must not be "a mechanic, artisan or laborer." The addition reflected a very different social structure and tradition which held the amateur and the gentleman to be synonymous. Both the English and the American definitions expressed their mutual concern that the amateur should avoid any of the financial entanglements which plagued professional rowing. However, amateur rowing in England was to remain an activity primarily for gentlemen, while in the American tradition rowing for pleasure should be available to anyone, regardless of how he earned his living. Over the next one hundred years, as international competition developed through the Olympics, the Anglo-American definition of amateur would eventually be challenged by a very different interpretation.

Meanwhile, during the nineteenth century heyday of American rowing the clubs represented the most popular and populous part. As the tide of popularity receded, only the stronger clubs survived: they were able to maintain the National Championships each year, as well as their local regattas and to keep alive the NAAO, which eventually voted in 1929 to include individual and college members in addition to amateur clubs. Survival was not easy. Industrialism would drive the New York clubs from the Harlem River to the less convenient waters of Orchard Beach Lagoon. In Boston the creation of the Basin in 1910 through the efforts of a Harvard oarsman—James Storrow, Class of 1885—made possible a new era in boating on the Charles. Fortunately, the clubs of the Schuylkill Navy were able to remain anchored on Boat House Row.

One of the clubs' most important contributions was to keep alive and flourishing the tradition of small boats in part because the strongest influence on their coaching was the old professional scullers. Unfortunately, with the latter's disappearance the two groups remaining in this country—the clubs and the college oarsmen—never achieved the same continuous reciprocal relationship which has long prevailed in England. Until quite recently the college oarsman rarely continued to row after graduation. Only the lucky colleges like Harvard, Columbia or Pennsylvania found club crews conveniently at hand for friendly rivalry. So college rowing developed slowly, discontinuously and almost in isolation.

Rowing Leads the Colleges into Intercollegiate Sports

Despite an early start rowing in American colleges took almost fifty years to become widely and firmly established. And its true flowering was not to come until after World War I and later. Less than ten years after Harvard and Yale undergraduates discovered the pleasures of boating, four crews met in 1852 at **Lake Winnepesaukee** in New Hampshire "to test the superiority of the oarsmen of the two colleges," in the words of the original challenge. Until 1871 the two raced only intermittently, usually on Lake Quinsigamond near Worcester, Massachusetts, for three miles with one turn. Out of the general enthusiasm for rowing in the 70s emerged the **Rowing Association of American Colleges.** Assembled at Harvard's invitation, the Association organized a series of intercollegiate regattas over the next six years. Since the race was a three mile straightaway, heats were impossible; so the Association kept searching for a place where many crews could race abreast. Since they were racing in VIs without cox, accidents and arguments were inescapable. At **Saratoga** in 1875, thirteen colleges—Cornell, Harvard, Yale, Columbia, Dartmouth, Wesleyan, Amherst, Brown, Williams, Bowdoin, Hamilton, Union and Princeton—raced before perhaps 25,000 people. Yale, who had won only one of the Association races and found them too crowded for good rowing, resigned from the Association and challenged Harvard, who resigned the next year, to a four mile race in VIIIs, a match race in imitation of Oxford and Cambridge who had been racing since 1829. After two races in Springfield, the race was moved to **New London** where it has been held annually ever since with very few exceptions.

The outburst of student interest in rowing in the decade after the Civil War
produced the Rowing Association of American Colleges. Only three crews finally
raced in its first regatta in 1871. Two years later eleven crews came to Saratoga
to race over the three-mile straightaway, with the encouragement of Saratoga's
hotel owners who welcomed the 25,000 spectators. The next year (pictured above)
nine Varsity crews finally came to the line after two days of wrangling and post-
ponements. Harvard and Yale collided at the two-mile flags, to leave Yale limping
home with a broken oar. Columbia's victory occupied the entired front page
of the *New York Times*.

The Association soon dissolved. Denied the chance to upset Harvard or
Yale, most other colleges gave up rowing in favor of more popular, less expensive sports. Over the next twenty years, Columbia, Cornell and Penn kept
trying either to get Harvard and Yale to let them into New London or to
start their own match races like the **Childs Cup** which begin in 1879. Almost twenty years later in 1895 they finally succeeded in organizing another
regatta over four miles for VIIIs at Poughkeepsie. The direct ancestor of the
present Intercollegiate Rowing Association, **Poughkeepsie** would gradually
evolve into a truly national regatta as other eastern crews (Syracuse 1901
and Navy 1907) as well as Wisconsin (1897), Stanford (1912), Washington
(1913) and California (1921) came aboard. In one sense the persistence of the
two alternatives—the match race or the regatta—served to inhibit the full
development of college rowing until after World War II. Although few match
races were inspired by the same institutional rivalry as with Harvard and Yale
or California and Washington, cup races or spring fixtures between two or

POUGHKEEPSIE REGATTA

INTERCOLLEGIATE
ROWING
ASSOCIATION
JUNE 25. 1941

25¢
OFFICIAL PROGRAM

Railroads and Rowing

The railroads and boat racing arrived in America about the same time. It was a conductor with a good eye for business who encouraged the first Harvard-Yale race at Winnepesaukee in 1852. From then to the coming of World War II, if there was a railroad running along the river or lake, a train of flat cars with seats for spectators appeared very quickly. New London, Ithaca, Lake Carnegie, Derby and Poughkeepsie, as this picture shows, would have a train of a dozen or more cars along the shore. And everyone always accused the engineer of trying to give himself the best seat!

three colleges did appear as preliminaries before Poughkeepsie or New London. (Harvard and Yale were wedded to their version of the Boat Race!) But as long as the four mile distance remained the ultimate test, heats were out of the question. So the earlier match races were rowed at every distance from a Henley to two miles; eventually Junior Varsity and Freshmen races were introduced; but work in small boats tended to disappear as endurance over distance became the ideal. Meanwhile, having ushered in the great age of intercollegiate sports, rowing was soon overshadowed by the others, even while it retained a kind of primacy which recognition of the effort involved and the virtual absence of any commercialism would always give it.

Other difficulties circumscribed the early development of rowing in American colleges. Expensive equipment, boathouses and an accessible body of water were some of the complications. In the early days the students were responsible for everything, with little more than grudging permission and no financial help from faculties and administrations for the first fifty years. In nineteenth-century American colleges the class was the great organizing unit, but it lacked the proper continuity for a boat club. Enthusiasm waned and the equipment deteriorated even before the class had graduated. An incoming class had to start from scratch. A college boat club like the Yale Navy was little better, with no box office income and dependent on student subscriptions—if they could get them—the generosity of other more lucrative sports like football or baseball, the benefits which the Banjo Club, the Glee Club or the Dramat might run for the Boat Club, and eventually the generous support of the rowing alumni. Colleges were still small. To find the $400 for a shell when a year's tuition was only $150, especially if the entire student body numbered less than five-hundred, was not easy. Often the shell and the crew went together on a flat car, cinders and all. Little wonder that in 1874 the Dartmouth shell caught fire in the Hoosic Tunnel on the way to the Association Regatta at Saratoga.

Finally, the weather, together with the academic calendar, has always complicated rowing in most American colleges. In England rowing at Oxford and Cambridge could be carried on virtually the year round, with a most stimulating mixture of boat races for every level of interest and ability. By contrast, most American colleges found their practice limited to a couple of months in the fall, the spring as soon as the ice went out, and the early summer. Only recently has a program of races for the fall emerged. So the college oarsman faced a cheerless prospect: hours of lonely fall practice; winter runs, weights in the gym, primitive hydraulic rowing machines, and after 1890 rowing tanks with dead water; and an all too short spring to get the crew ready for the one or perhaps two races of the year. A baseball or football team was infinitely easier to move around by rail and develop the kind of busy, competitive schedule that helped to make a team or crew, as well as attract public interest and support.

The Evolution
of American Orthodox

In the evolution of rowing style in this country, the colleges have always played an important part. The basic problem is simple: how best to lever the boat through the water, by applying most effectively arms, back and legs to the blade while it is in the water and interfering as little as possible with the run of the boat during the rest of the stroke. Technology, of course, is of critical importance in shaping a style, whether it is the weight and shape of boat and oars or their rig. As long as rowing was on fixed seats, the back and arms could be put to work much more completely than the legs. Of necessity the answer included a pronounced back-swing from the hips and a comparatively high rate of striking. Even though the sliding seat would eventually make the legs the most important part of the stroke, this very fact made the harnessing of back, arms and slide both critically important and inevitably controversial: the earlier importance of the back-swing yielded place only slowly and grudgingly to the superior strength of the leg-drive. The original slides were less than 6-inches long, and the oarsman was stopped back of his work by several inches. Only after the mid-80s was he coming up to the pin on a 16-inch slide. In many ways it was the newly acquired wealth of resources made available by the slide which eventually gave rise to the variations in style as different sequences for harnessing the back, arms and legs to the oar now became possible.

With the emergence of different styles, how they were handed down became important. There has always been a natural style to the extent that through trial and error individuals, especially scullers, have often discovered the most effective way to move a boat. The young Charles Courtney, for instance, had apparently come upon the most efficient stroke for himself during the long hours of lonely practice on Cayuga Lake off his native village of Union Springs. As has already been seen, Courtney and other professionals eventually became successful coaches of college crews, thus perpetuating the natural, scullers' style. To it was joined an import from England, whose influence on American rowing was the most formative in the nineteenth-century.

The first formal rowing style, **English Orthodox,** had appeared in answer to the technical problems of the fixed-seat and as an expression of nineteenth-century England. Many of the public schools—Eton, Westminster, Shrewsbury, Radley—and the two ancient universities were conveniently located on enticing rivers where rowing was possible almost the year round. Academic programs which featured the humanist ideal of *mens sana in corpore sano*, as well as the social utility of competitive sports completed the idyllic setting for painstakingly teaching boys and young men the nice points of style, especially a physically demanding body swing with a straight back swinging from the hips. By the middle of the century, oarsmen and coaches were articulating the details of the Orthodox style, largely in reaction against the rather short swing and early break of the arms which professional watermen had originally developed with their heavier work boats. English Orthodox originated on fixed seats, and many of its disciples remained convinced that all oarsmen should be started out on them. As between slide and body swing, it has always emphasized a shorter slide and a longer swing. This puts the shoulders well back at the open finish where the wrists and hands drop squarely and smartly, to lead the arms, body and slide into a definitely sequential recovery, with the slide not starting forward until the hands have crossed the knees and de-accelerating as it approaches the front stop. A sharp, quick beginning is taken with the legs and shoulders opening up together and arms being saved for the second half of the stroke. At first American oarsmen learned of English Orthodox through books. By 1870 the literature on rowing style was considerable, almost all of it originating in England as was long to be the case. *The Principles of Rowing at Harvard*, published by the Harvard University Boat Club in 1873 for fifty-cents a copy and one of the first American treatises on style, was freely adopted from an English work of twenty years before.

That same year **Bob Cook,** then a sophomore and captain at Yale, became convinced that, in his words, "there was really no one in America who understood the subject . . . Reading descriptions and conversing with one or two English varsity men had given me a faint idea of what their stroke was. I felt convinced that Yale had to go to school in rowing and learn her alphabet." The result of his three months of studying rowing at London, Cambridge and Oxford was the migration of English Orthodox to America, just at the mo-

The Harvard pamphlet of 44 pages emphasized "a rational method of teaching" and the attaining of "form and swing," much preferable to "bucketing in a six-oar amid shouts and abuse."

ment when the sliding seat was making a review of that style necessary. With a shorter rowing season and virtually no comparable secondary school feeders where a boy could master the long, straight-backed body swing and the fixed pin, the changes in the English import to suit American conditions were as predictable as they were necessary: a shorter swing on longer slides; swivels instead of fixed pins; larger blades; center-seating and shorter oars inboard; fast hands out of bow, blade low on the recovery and often a slower entry. But American Orthodox would keep essentially the same finish, recovery and ratio if not the body swing of the English original.

Although initially greeted with much chauvinistic suspicion as an effete import from England, the new **American Orthodox** eventually caught on, particularly after Courtney and other sculler-coaches had securely fixed the leg drive in the middle of the stroke. Over the next forty years American Orthodox kept in touch with its English origins in various ways. In the 90s both Courtney and Cook took crews to Henley. Though unsuccessful, both seem to have realized that by shortening the body swing at both ends of the stroke the latter might in fact become too short. The occasional importation of English amateur coaches to Harvard, Yale and Penn in the years before 1914 represented additional infusions of the true faith, again with no remarkable success since American colleges, their students and their ways continued to mystify these visitors.

Perhaps the most permanent, extensive adaptation of the English tradition to American conditions came through **Hiram Conibear** at the University of Washington. In the spring of 1907 the former trainer of the White Sox and Alonzo Stagg's football team at the University of Chicago coached his first crew at Seattle. Brought to Washington to train the football team, Conibear took over the crew almost on a wager. His training for the job included a few hours of rowing at Chautauqua summer sessions, careful study of an English book on rowing, and some now legendary experiments the previous winter. With a skeleton borrowed from the biology laboratory he learned for himself the anatomical movement which a stroke required of an oarsman: where, how and when the maximum drive could be applied to the oar. Similarly, by keeping a bicycle wheel spinning steadily with a simple pat of his hand, he came upon the critical role of the recovery in maintaining a steady run to a shell. His Chautauqua coach had been a pupil of Bob Cook. The **Pocock Brothers**, whom Conibear persuaded to move down from Vancouver, gave

In Hiram Conibear (1871–1917) energy, ambition and optimism were nicely balanced by his practical, versatile hand, his incisive mind and his fearless, rough but never unkind tongue. To the University authorities who were set on firing him, he once said: "Don't fire me, please. We're on to something really worthwhile here."

him another contact with English Orthodoxy. Soon to become the principal builders of shells to American crews for more than a half century, the brothers hailed from a family of watermen at Eton College, an historic center of Orthodoxy. Conibear's genius was to discover and absorb the central elements of English Orthodox and then adapt them to American conditions and physiques, to develop a native American style, something which neither Cook nor Courtney had quite been able to do.

Killed in a tragic accident in 1917 when only forty-six and barely ten years into his chosen vocation, Conibear left an almost legendary style and a dynasty of pupils to carry it across the country. His successor at Washington, **Ed Leader,** rowed 2 in the Husky crew which confounded the experts to take third at Poughkeepsie in 1913. Ten years later Leader moved east to Yale, the first example of an American oarsman-graduate who chose coaching as his profession and bellwether of a Washington invasion which would spread the Washington perfection of American Orthodox throughout the country: in 1925 **Ky Ebright,** Washington's cox in 1915-16-17, began his thirty-five years of coaching at California; **Rusty Callow,** captain of the 1915 crew, followed Leader at Washington, was called to Pennsylvania in 1927 and finally moved to Navy in 1950. Among Callow's pupils at Seattle a second generation of Washington coaches soon appeared: **Al Ulbrickson,** who stroked Callow's last three Washington crews, succeeded his mentor there, while his classmates, **Stork Stanford** and **Tom Bolles** were eventually lured east in 1936 to coach at Cornell and Harvard. By 1937 every major rowing college in the country, save Columbia, Navy and Syracuse, enjoyed the benefits of a Washington coach, a pupil either of Conibear himself or of Rusty Callow. And after World War II a third generation of Washington coaches began to emerge.

Like so much else in American rowing, the emergence of the professional coach was as much determined by technological developments as by the absence of available gentlemen amateurs. On lakes and rivers a coaching launch is essential. Yet a gasoline launch capable of keeping up with an VIII was not available until after World War I. Steam launches appeared in the 1880s, but their limitations were all too obvious: starting was slow; their fuel was heavy and bulky; the early ones could not keep up with a crew; and in spite of their expense they were always breaking down. In April, 1907 Courtney had to keep steam up night and day on the *Cornell* to prevent her boiler, condenser and pipes from freezing. In an earlier day the coach might actually row with the crew or coach from a sculling boat. In 1873 one of the most valuable ideas Cook brought back from England was the tub-pair for coaching, equally useful in helping the beginner with fundamentals or in allowing a coach to work quietly with a Varsity oarsman on some refinement which might be troubling the perfection of the University crew. Until the coming of the professional coach, the captain was responsible not only for picking the style, the coach and the crew, but also for much of the coaching, all of which often proved to be more responsibility than one man could carry and still row very well himself. Interestingly enough, the manager in some form or other had appeared long before the professional coach, for there were always details of logistics, rigging and even fund-raising to be dumped on him!

With the spread of the Washington version of American Orthodox throughout the country between the wars there prevailed perhaps a greater uniformity of style and stability of technology and training than ever before or since. All were concerned to have the power come on immediately without missing water, to build up the drive to a solid finish, to get the crew out of bow quickly with fast hands and shoulders coming over, to slow down the slide as it approached the front stop yet to avoid any hang. Throughout there was meticulous attention to wrists, blade work and body swing, in the belief that uniformity inboard and timing would maximize the power being applied to the blade. Selecting a crew was a special problem for these coaches, partly because they were always impatient to get the order set so that the crew's precision and polish could be worked on. But the ergometer had not yet appeared, and the use of small boats to compare the different oarsmen's ability to move a boat was generally ignored. So there remained innumerable three-minute runs between two boats; after each run the boats came together to change a couple of men; then another run until such exhausting trial and error seemed to have produced the best combination.

Perhaps the best evidence of the success of college coaches is seen in the Olympics. Starting with the Navy in 1920, American college VIIIs won eight successive Olympic gold medals, with California actually winning three times. The responsibility for small boats, however, was left almost entirely to the clubs. In the Olympics before World War II the clubs provided American crews each time for three or four other medals, usually in the singles and double sculls, the pair and IV with cox. All too few college oarsmen kept up their rowing after college, in part because few of them had learned to row in anything but an VIII. Unfortunately for the long term health of rowing in this country, the colleges, their oarsmen and coaches remained in only intermittent contact at best with the clubs, meeting every four years almost as strangers on the occasion of the Olympic trials. The persistence of an almost national Washington style perhaps prevented as much experiment as was taking place elsewhere. And the persistence of a great variety of college races from the Henley to four miles perpetuated an almost mystical belief that mileage was the best if not the only way to produce a winning crew. Infinite attention to such inboard refinements as how a man carried his elbows could confuse means with ends and miss the way the blade was moving the water. Confident in the superiority of its style and boasting the finest physical material in the world, American rowing, especially in the colleges, remained

All year the goal had been "a California crew for California's Olympics." Victors at Poughkeepsie, Cal beat an older, more experienced Penn A. C. boat in the Trials by one-fifth of a second. This cliff-hanger proved useful training for the Olympic Finals at Long Beach (note the oil wells!). A heavier, older Italian crew in the more sheltered lane never rowed below 39, with USA 3 or 4 strokes lower for the first 1000 meters. Both crews went to 40 and over; the lead see-sawed and the USA won by three-feet, the second of three Olympic victories for California and its coach, Ky Ebright.

comparatively oblivious to the veritable revolution in technology, technique and training which intensified competition at the international level was bringing.

American Rowing in Its Second Century

In the thirty years since World War II American rowing has enjoyed more activity, more popularity and a broader base than at anytime since its first years a century ago. Surprisingly enough, there has been a rush of new developments in boats and rigging, much of it from abroad. Shovel or spade blades, moveable buttons and adjustable riggers have now combined to permit the easy readjustment of inboard-outboard ratios to match variations in weather, boats and oarsmen. New materials are making possible lighter and stronger shells. The importance of accommodating rig to the individual oarsman to make his rowing of maximum effectiveness is recognized as never before.

With the new equipment has come another style of rowing, **International Modern** or **Ratzeburg,** named after the little German town forty kilometers northeast of Hamburg. By 1962 its Boat Club had won or shared in thirteen German, three European, one World Championship and two Olympic titles, under the informed, inspired leadership of **Karl Adam,** a teacher in the local secondary school. By coincidence it had been the victories as early as 1933 of a Fairbairn-trained crew over Germany's best which raised doubts about the prevailing Orthodox style, especially since the latter had increasingly concentrated on body posture at the expense of moving the boat. **Steven Fairbairn (1862–1938),** a most articulate Australian critic of traditional Orthodoxy, had taught: "Drive at your blade and let your body and slide take care of themselves." It was Fairbairn that helped Adam and his colleagues to their own revision of Orthodoxy which culminated in the victory of the West German crew at the Rome Olympics in 1960, the first time in forty years an American VIII had not won the Olympics.

In the last fifteen years the Ratzeburg style has spread the world over, including the United States. As a style it is perhaps more closely linked to certain developments in technique, training and even equipment than was the case in any previous style. At Ratzeburg Karl Adam sought equal perfection of technique, strength and stamina, all of which were essential for a superior crew. Technically his first concern was to obtain as constant hull speed as possible, with the minimum contrast between drive and recovery. Indeed, its recovery represents the most radical departure from English or American Orthodox. Rather than a slow-down of the slide as it approaches the front stop, there is actually an increase in momentum in order to secure a quicker initial drive and a comparatively modest swing to anchor the blade. Though the stroke remains an unbroken cycle without pause, the Ratzeburg style produces an almost imperceptible gather in the middle of the recovery, visible only at a lower rating but serving to unite the crew for the swing into the catch. Ratings tend to be higher than American Orthodox had once preferred. Over 2000 meters, the basic distance for all international racing, the crews usually race at a cadence of 37 to 42, depending on the competition and the conditions of wind and water.

Once the technique has been mastered, strength and stamina become of prime importance for the International Modern style. A crew's training—how it is conditioned physically and psychologically—has changed most dramatically in the last twenty-five years. In contrast with the barbaric practices and superstitions of a century ago, diet has become sensible and uncomplicated. The time when boils were the oarsman's worst enemy lies not so far back; true understanding of germ theory and careful attention to the cleanliness of equipment and clothes have done even more than wonder drugs to virtually eliminate this menace. Impure, dirty drinking water is no longer the peril it once was. Both land training and water training have benefited from the latest advances in physiology, kinesiology and even psychology which have so effectively partnered the Ratzeburg style. Oarsmen, following the lead of swimmers and runners, are profiting from the enormous advances in scientific and medical knowledge about what makes Sammy run (or row) fast and how to build up his circulation, muscles and endurance so that he can row faster.

Work on the water is both longer and more carefully planned than before. In this country competitive rowing now has three seasons: spring, summer and fall. The list of fixtures rivals that of a century ago in number and ranges over the whole country. A new kind of regatta or race like the **Head of the Charles** has made it possible for hundreds of crews of all sorts and abilities to race in procession over three miles against the clock, thus providing much-needed color and interest for fall rowing and pointing up the simple truth that "mileage is a means to an end and not an end in itself." The variety of

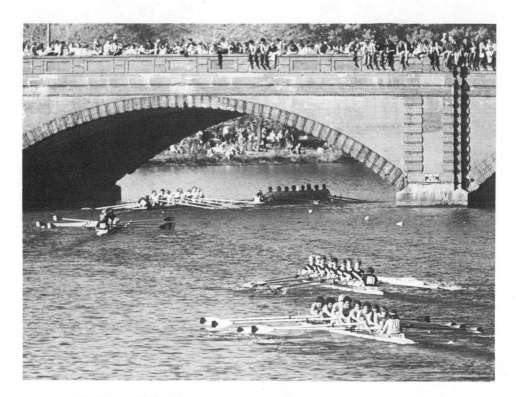

The Youth VIIIs at the 1978 Head of the Charles Crowd Through the
Anderson Bridge

Now (1980) in its sixteenth year the Head of the Charles has become one of the
most exciting, festive events of the rowing year and the model for a host of Heads
across the country. At the Charles over 3000 rowers and 720 shells from all over
America race in 18 different events from 9:30 A.M. to 4:00 P.M. Each limited to
40 entries, the events include singles, doubles, pairs, IVs with and VIIIs, open to
rowers of different ability and age. Three of the races are exclusively for women,
while they join men in the mixed VIIIs. The events are spaced 15 to 30 minutes
apart. Within each race the 40 crews start one after another at 10 to 15 second
intervals and chase each other up river for three miles. Thanks to the computer,
each crew's elapsed time and the order of finish can be announced within 15
minutes. Meanwhile, the thousands lining the banks and crowding the bridges
are enjoying rowing at its best—and for fun.

distances over which American college crews traditionally raced has been
almost completely replaced by the 2000 meter Olympic distance. In part the
change was inspired by the need for American crews to prepare better to
compete internationally at 2000 meters. Concentration on a single distance
also makes training more precise and a crew's progress more measurable.
Thus, **interval training** of, for instance, six sprints over 500 meters against
the clock to duplicate a fixed time can combine speed-training and
endurance-training which will eventually increase the crew's speed over 2000

bassin ile notre-dame   july 24 juil   11:55   resultants / results
aviron   une rameuse   femmes finale 1-6   course/race no: 74
rowing   single-scull   women   final 1-6
                                      date/hr: 24/12:04   fin: if

rg coul rk lane			250 m	500 m	750 m	1000 m
1	2	gdr	87 scheiblich, christine 0:58.21 (2)	1:59.16 (1) +1:00.95	3:02.26 (1) +1:03.10	4:05.56 +1:03.30
2	6	usa	230 lind, joan 0:58.99 (4)	1:59.63 (2) +1:00.64	3:03.68 (2) +1:04.05	4:06.21 +1:02.53
3	1	urs	187 antonova, elena 0:58.57 (3)	2:01.00 (3) +1:02.43	3:05.97 (3) +1:04.97	4:10.24 +1:04.27
4	5	bul	12 spassova, rossitza 1:01.17 (6)	2:02.83 (5) +1:01.66	3:09.05 (5) +1:06.22	4:10.86 +1:01.81
5	3	hol	121 munneke, ingrid 0:57.83 (1)	2:01.18 (4) +1:03.35	3:08.51 (4) +1:07.33	4:18.71 +1:10.20
6	4	hun	130 ambrus, mariann 1:00.19 (5)	2:04.40 (6) +1:04.21	3:14.12 (6) +1:09.72	4:22.59 +1:08.47

starter: o'hea   arbitres: schug
aligneur: hamilton   referes: schug
temps/weather: couvert/overcast
vent/wind: veloc. = 3, 1 m/s   comp. = -3,1 m/s   direction = n
temperature   air = 23.0 c   eau/water = 22,0 c
humidite/air humidity: 65 pc   pression atm./air pressure: 759 mm hg

Grand Finale Women's VIIIs, Montreal Olympics, 1976

With interval training for races over a set distance, interval timing has become critical. Fortunately, electronics can provide the answer: extremely precise timing of each separate crew at regular intervals. The above chart of the "splits" every 250 meters shows the battle for the medals between the USA and Russia (URS).

meters. This represents a considerable advance from the spring of 1883 when the Yale crew was made to race four miles every day for five weeks! By race day the stroke was so overtrained that they could not get the rating over 38 even though in practice, rowing a short stroke, they had never dropped below 42 for four miles.

Again **land-training** has acquired a new range, intensity and scientific purpose. Strength and stamina are sought through distance-running, bike-ergs, the ergometer, cross-country skiing, cycling, and specialized exercises with weights, all carefully logged, monitored and scheduled. With the ergometer the original, primitive rowing machine has been so perfected that it provides objective strength and endurance tests both for measuring and extending the capacity of the individual oarsman and for identifying, evaluating and comparing oarsmen of promise. The demands on the individual in such a program are truly awesome. It is little wonder that one participant confessed that "having fun" was the most difficult part of the goal to attain. As Karl Adam has written, the point is finally reached where motivation becomes the limiting factor, to use an old phrase, "the weakest link in the chain."

Perhaps the most dramatic aspect of the present renaissance in American rowing is its ever-broadening base. All over the country, in clubs, schools and colleges, men and women, young and old, heavy or light are learning to appreciate the challenge of rowing as well as the satisfaction and sense of well-being rowing provides. Many regattas are truly national, open to men and women of varying ability through novice, intermediate and elite divisions. Over a century ago rowing worked its way down from the colleges to the secondary schools, at first to the independent schools of the northeast which early on became persuaded of the social and personal values organized sports offered their charges. In time clubs and colleges worked to build a younger, broader base for the sport by providing coaching and equipment to local highschools and staging schoolboy regattas. In 1933 national championships were begun. With the addition of Junior programs, Youth Rowing now sends teams abroad to the international **FISA Youth Championships.**

Similarly, women have rowed for at least ninety years, on their own or at a few schools and colleges. In 1888 **Mollie King,** "oarswoman of Newport, Kentucky," issued a challenge to any "female" in Covington, Cincinnati or Newport for "a two mile race for stakes." As long as violent, competitive exercise for women was generally considered dangerous and unladylike, Mollie could not have received many challenges. Rowing for women was recreational and intramural; victory was decided on form rather than speed. After such tentative beginnings the dramatic appearance of women racing in the last fifteen years represents one of the most remarkable achievements of today's women's revolution. Organized in 1964, the **National Women's Rowing Association (NWRA)** drew only 45 boats and less than 100 competitors at its first regatta two years later. At Seattle in 1978, however, the **NWRA** boated 650 participants in 130 shells from 60 clubs. Overcoming their share of chauvinistic resistance which sometimes begrudged them boats, money and even water to row on, American women have "embraced rowing with astonishing fervor." As one of them has explained it: "They know that rowing is explosively and wildly physical, fiercely competitive and gracefully, delicately beautiful." Women's rowing has proved an international phenomenon in which American women joined almost from the start. By 1975 an American VIII took the silver in the **FISA Championships.** At the 1976 Olympics **Joan Lind's** silver in the sculls and the bronze by the VIII justified the verdict, again by a woman, that "women's rowing is the freshest, most innovative and by far the fastest growing aspect of American rowing, and at an international level, currently the most successful.

Ever since the first American sculler, **Edward Smith** from New York's Atlanta Club, had a try for the Diamonds at Henley, American amateurs have sought to measure themselves against international competition. Each year

Six years of dedicated, often lonely training lay between Joan Lind's first outing in a wherry at the Long Beach Rowing Association and the Olympic Silver Medal at Montreal in 1976. Her coach, parents, and club mates gave invaluable support, but ahead lay fall races for two and a half miles around the harbor islands, four or more intervals of 750 meters each day against the clock, weights and six-mile runs twice a week in the winter and countless races at home and aborad. Conditioning, endurance, and technique were all essential, but the fine tuning of her desire to prove herself and her ability to come back from defeat meant the difference.

over twenty American scullers or crews follow in his wake to the Thames valley market town which has become a favorite racing distance the world over. At the moment the fastest times in eight of the twelve events at the Royal Henley are held by crews from outside Great Britain for whom it has become a veritable Mecca. The **Canadian Henley**, about to celebrate its Centennial, has always welcomed American crews. It is the Olympics, how-

In 1938 Joe Burk, sculling 39 over the last half of the course, broke the Henley record for the Diamonds which had stood for 33 years. His style and training were very prophetic of the Ratzeburg or International Style which was to develop after the war. Burk's record stood for 27 years, but the new record lasted only 10, testifying to the more intensive international competition of today.

ever, and in recent years the European and World Championships, which have provided the most exacting test and challenge for American rowers.

In 1900 rowing was first included in the second of the modern Olympic Games. It was only in 1920 at Antwerp that six of the eventual seven rowing events finally appeared, although American crews had already won six gold medals in 1900 and 1904. In eight successive Olympics—from 1920 through 1956—a crew from an American university took the gold in the VIIIs. During that period the Americans were winning two or three other medals in each Olympics—a total of twenty-nine medals (17 gold, 5 silver and 7 bronze) or 52% of the best possible score (a medal in every race; there was no race for pair without in 1920). They had won the gold at least once in every event except the IV without. Throughout these years the college crews tended to concentrate on the VIIIs in the Trials, usually leaving the small boats to the clubs. In some of these Olympics the European countries were still recovering from the ravages of war, and after World War I the Central Powers were not allowed to compete again until 1928. Yet the achievement of the American crews was truly outstanding.

In the 1956 Olympics the USA VIII, having lost to Canada and Australia in the first heat, had to come back through the repechage to meet the same two crews in the finals. The U.S. beat Canada by a half length, to keep alive the string of U.S. victories in the VIIIs which Navy had started in 1920. As the picture shows, the effort required by the second Yale crew to represent the USA was considerable.

In retrospect, the coming of change is first visible at **Melbourne in 1956.** Six medals for the Americans, including golds in the pair with, pair without and the VIII, was a record, but the Russians took four, with golds in the sculls and the doubles. Over the next three years Karl Adam, his Ratzeburg crews, their training, style and rig began to win everything in the European Championships except the sculls. The day of reckoning came in 1960, at Lake Albano in the Rome Olympics. America was represented by one of its strongest teams—five out of seven crews made the finals. Yet one gold and one bronze were the end result. Meanwhile, Russia, with six crews in the finals, won three golds, one silver and one bronze, while Germany with five finalists was gaining three golds and a silver. Lake Albano also saw record times in five finals, impressive proof of the new level of competition produced by the remarkable improvement in European rowing.

Over the next few years, America, its coaches and its oarsmen went back to school under the leadership of the Olympic Committee. The implications for physically conditioning a crew, for style, for equipment and even for the traditional American view of sport in society had all to be re-examined. In

1963 firsthand evidence of what had to be done was provided by the six-week visit of a Ratzeburg VIII. Undefeated in six races except in a heat of the Eastern Sprints, they beat Cornell, the best of the East, in the finals by a good length, rowing 40 most of the way. The times were calling for a new kind of cooperation between clubs and colleges: a rowing center strategically located, well-equipped and prepared to be supportive both afloat and ashore. The **Lake Washington Boat Club** was found in 1958 for this purpose, and across the continent **Vesper,** found almost a century earlier, stood ready to provide the model.

Cheerfully accepting the old truism that "if you can't lick 'em, join 'em," Vesper and the veteran Olympic sculler, **Jack Kelly,** proceeded to package a representative VIII: experienced oarsmen from different colleges and clubs, willing to work 'together for a year, under a coach who had himself rowed for Karl Adam and was ready to try Ratzeburg's weight training, land training and interval training. Prophetic in their makeup of the **National Camp** which lay ten years in the future, the crew won the Trials handily and led a team to the Tokyo Olympics which did much to recover America's self-confidence and reputation. Again five American crews made the finals, but this time two golds, a silver and a bronze showed that the lesson was being learned. The VIII won over Germany by open water, and **Conn Findlay** took his third medal in the pair with (gold in 1956, bronze in 1960 and gold in 1964). Yet the old order was never to return; the Germans figured in six finals and took four medals—one gold, two silver and a bronze—while the Russians won two gold in five finals. After 1956 the Olympic course had six lanes, and thus six finalists in every event.

By 1968 and the Mexican Olympics the new situation with international rowing, as with most sports, came clear. Many countries, especially those behind the Iron Curtain, saw sport as a concern for the state, too important to be left to its own devices. An all-embracing department of government to provide uniformity, direction and purpose was to raise the level of rowing competition as much as interval training had done a decade earlier. Teams representing the two Germanies appeared for the first time in 1968. Immediately East Germany began to show what totalitarian centralization could produce. Out of a population of seventeen million came six finalists and two golds and a silver; by contrast America with seven finalists came up with a silver and a bronze. A pattern was emerging which would prevail at Munich in 1972 and at Montreal in 1976. While America had to rest content with one silver each time, the East Germans would continue to set an awesome pace, with seven medals out of seven finals in 1972 and seven medals out of eight finals in 1976 (a new event—the quad—had been added). Yet the competition became more extensive as well as intensive, as the following table makes clear:

	1968	*1972*	*1976*
No. of Countries in the Finals	16	14	17
No. of Countries Winning Medals	12	10	9

Just as the number of countries winning medals kept shrinking, so the general level of competition was expanding. In an effort to gear up for this higher level, the NAAO has been trying to send crews to the European or World Championships since the early 60s. The opportunity to row against Olympic caliber oarsmen at these regattas can provide invaluable racing experience. Indeed, one reason for the rapid improvement in American women's rowing has been their readiness to submit to the unpleasant realities of international competition. Just one year after the first NWRA regatta, an American VIII rowed at Vichy in the FISA European Championships. Sixth place, while quite creditable, showed how far they had to go. Annual trips abroad finally bore fruit in the two medals won by American women at **Montreal in 1976,** the first time women's rowing was included in the Olympics.

While more successful than American men, the women encountered the same formidable opposition. East Germany took four gold and two silver medals out of the six races. Over 77% of the medals were won by East Germany, Russia and Bulgaria, all countries where the government had decided to make sport an arm of national policy.

This intensification of international rivalry is setting a standard of performance which is becoming increasingly difficult for individual Americans to meet without extraordinary personal sacrifices in time and careers, sacrifices which amateur oarsmen, at least in this country, have never been called upon to make. Similarly, the NAAO, the National Olympic Committee and the federal government must decide how best to meet this state-mobilized challenge. A selection process based simply on the traditional division of club and colleges is probably not going to mobilize the best American rowers for today's level of international competition. And only America's best can hope to compete successfully at this level. Some kind of **National Team,** however new and disturbing to existing arrangements, is the only answer. So far the **NAAO** has shown the flexibility and imagination to adjust to the changing situation. For over forty years schools and colleges have been encouraged to share membership with the clubs. Now room must be made for women's rowing and the new type of club which arises out of the development programs. The breadth of national interest in rowing must be effectively mobilized with a new regional organization. The depth required to race successfully at the international level needs money if Americans rather than

America is to provide the proper support for the country's rowing. Perhaps the most hopeful sign for American rowing, even if it has no easy answer to the above questions, is the ever-increasing interest in getting afloat in some kind or combination of shell.

Epilogue

Rowing shared, even led, in the coming of sport to American society. Yet the very nature of the sport has given it a distinct development of its own which defies the easy generalizations of the sociologist or historian. As with all games, rowing's original basic appeal was as a release from everyday life, "the purest form of escape." Since its first professional phase was short-lived, the sport escaped the degradation that commercialism has meant for other sports, turning "play into work" and subordinating "the athlete's pleasure to the spectator's." Rowing has avoided such contamination of standards as baseball's designated hitter and has been able to maintain that "staged rivalry of superior ability" which gives athletics their imaginative appeal and brings out over 3,000 rowers, 700 crews and 50,000 spectators to the **Head of the Charles** each October. Early on rowing demonstrated its possibilities in character-building as preparation for life. Few sports continue to give expression to the competitive urge while still helping to discipline it by measuring "individual achievement against abstract standards of excellence," encouraging "cooperation among team mates" and enforcing "rules of fair play." Like all sports, however, rowing risks losing its charm when forced into the service of national rivalry, education, character development or social improvement.

The appeal of rowing, now well into its second century in America, continues to mystify those who have so far resisted its spell. Except for a few Heads, it hardly ranks high as a spectator sport. The physical and psychic demands which rowing makes on any serious participant put it near the top of any list, while the cost of equipment makes rowing almost elitist for many people. Yet more men and women today are discovering satisfaction and pleasure, however mysterious or inexplicable, in rowing than ever before. For the single sculler it may be the successful timing of a complex cycle of muscular movements as he savors the utter isolation of the sculler, so immediately dependent on his own efforts. For the oarsman who is rowing with someone else, the challenge of the timing is now compounded by the necessity of synchronizing his own timing with the rest of the crew. Whatever the combination, the rewards of physical fitness, the chance for personal growth and greater self-knowledge and for some the pleasure of just "messing around in boats" will keep bringing them out. Over thirty years ago an English coach remarked that "rowing is not a game. . . . The dictionary will not let you either play or play at rowing." So it continues, unique among sports and—when the boat is truly moving—a veritable religious experience for its devotees.

Bibliography

The history of rowing is an inseparable part of the history of sport, no matter how distinctive the former may have been. The following list, short, selective and subjective, assumes that anyone interested in further reading on rowing will wish at least to have a look at the larger picture. Some of the books suggested are out of print, but may be found in large libraries or second-hand bookstores.

The volume of literature on sport in general has only recently begun to match the place of sport in American society. So far much of the writing consists of how-to manuals, lurid novels, awe-struck biographies or as-told-to memoirs of sports heroes. Only in the last decade have the sociologists, philosophers and belatedly the historians joined the journalists, not so much to chronicle an event or a season but rather to analyze sport, its nature and appeal as well as its role in American society. By now every kind of writer or writing has come aboard. Jogging, for instance, has swept the bookstores almost as fast as it ran across the country. From head to foot, from soul to shin-splint, with plenty of attention to heart, lungs and stomach along the way, nothing has escaped the writers' pen and the publishers' list.

For several reasons rowing has so far escaped the literary avalanche. Its great popularity with the general public lies far in the past, just at the beginning of mass-sport. Even though the number and enthusiasm of its participants are greater than ever before, the sport can continue to avoid the more destructive pressures of commercialism, professionalism, and publishers' row. Boring for the uninitiated, mystifying to the non-participant, a secular reli-

49

gion for those who have felt its spell, rowing has so far produced little in the way of literature, especially in the United States by comparison with England.

I. The History of Sport: it seemed most useful to arrange this selection chronologically.

1. Krout, John A. *Annals of American Sport.* New Haven: Yale, 1929. This pioneer survey has become a classic. The growth of sport in every aspect, from competitive games to the outdoor movement, is skillfully projected against the general narrative of American history. A part of the *Pageant of America* series, the book includes many pictures, a good index and a useful bibliography.

2. Dulles, Foster R. *America Learns to Play* (reprinted Gloucester MA: Peter Smith, 1959). Originally published in 1940, the book is a history of organized popular public recreation from 1607 to 1940. Dulles was very impressed by two factors: first, the "continuous influence of an inherent Puritanism" which helped to form the American tradition that even amusements should at least pretend to serve "socially useful ends"; and second, the degree to which industrialism and urbanism had fostered "an ever growing need for play" as met by spectator sports. A good index, notes and a bibliography make the book particularly useful.

3. Betts, John R. *America's Sporting Heritage.* Reading, MA: Addison-Wesley, 1974. A very useful, scholarly, social and cultural history of sport in the United States from 1850 to 1950. In the transformation of class sport into mass sport the history of rowing is related to the more general history of sport.

4. Michener, James A. *Sports in America.* New York: Random House, 1976. A kaleidoscopic survey of the place of sports in contemporary American life. Sports and health, their financing, the role of the media, women in sports, international competition in sports, the misuse as well as the use of sports are just some of the topics which come under the author's dissecting hand. Except as it might relate to these more general topics, rowing figures only in the section on sports and health.

5. Twombly, Wells. *200 Years of Sport in America.* New York: McGraw Hill, 1976. A pleasant, well-illustrated book.

6. Lucas, John A. and Smith, Ronald A. *A Saga of American Sport.* Philadelphia: Lea and Feibiger, 1978. An historical survey which interprets sport "as a reflection of the dominant ideological themes in emerging throughout the course of American history."

7. Murphy, Cullen and others, "Sports in America," *The Wilson Quarterly*, Vol. II Summer, 1979, 56–87. A lively survey of the growth of sport in the United States since the Civil War, with an estimate of the impact of television on sport, some speculation on sport and the American character and a useful bibliographical essay.

II. Sport and Society: Even the few titles which follow give some indication of the bewildering range of inquiry which is now focused on sport. The classic formula which equated sport with character building has been shattered and remade past all recognition. Sport and freedom, is it to be found in individual sports or team sports? Sports and leisure, sports as a business, sports and social mobility? These are just some of the questions which sociologists, historians and philosophers are seeking to answer.

8. Talamini, John T. and Page, Charles H., ed. *Sport and Society: An Anthology.* Boston: Little Brown, 1973. A collection of readings on different aspects of sport in modern society.

9. Novak, Michael. *The Joy of Sport.* New York: Basic Books, 1976. Convinced that sports have become a religion for many Americans, the author examines both the heresies and the orthodoxies. In particular he is realistic about the two levels of the American mythology of sports: the Frank Merriwell belief in sport as preparation for the game of

life as opposed by the prevalence of commercialism, corruption and machismo among participants and fans.

10. Edwards, Harry. *The Sociology of Sport*. Homewood, Ill.: The Dorsey Press, 1973. An extensive analysis of sport as a social institution in America, including the coach, the fan, the athlete (black and white), and the relation of sport to social change.

11. Guttman, Allen. *From Ritual to Record*. New York: Columbia University Press, 1978. The author has singled out seven characteristics whose emergence is responsible for modern sport: secularism, equality, specialization, rationalization, bureaucracy, quantification, and records. Although rowing is mentioned only in passing, it is interesting how many of these characteristics have overtaken rowing in the last half century.

12. Weiss, Paul. *Sport: A Philosophic Inquiry*. Carbondale, Ill.: Sou. Illinois Press, 1969. A professional philosopher and by his own admission no athlete, Weiss examined sport in his search for philosophical principles. Viewing sport and games as something more than man at play, Weiss concluded that "athletics is mind displayed in a body well made, set in particular situations, involved in struggles, and performing in games."

III. Rowing—Bibliography and Journals: With the exception of a short bibliography in Cleaver (18), the most complete bibliography on rowing is Brittain's as reprinted and brought up to 1940 in Herrick (23). Fortunately, both the British (ARA) and American (NAA) rowing associations maintain very useful journals. As befits such a venerable sport, except for the Jockey Club, they are the oldest organizations of the sort in their countries and probably the world; the ARA was founded in 1861, the NAAO nine years later.

14. *The Oarsman*, the official publication of the National Association of Amateur Oarsmen has been published six times a year since 1968. In addition to national and international regatta results, *The Oarsman* contains articles on coaching, training equipment and history. It is sent to all members of the NAAO; separate subscriptions ($20.00 a year) may be requested from the Executive Secretary, NAAO, No. 4 Boathouse Row, Philadelphia, PA 19130.

15. *British Rowing Almanack*, the official year book of the ARA contains regatta results as well as articles and reports. It can be obtained from the ARA, 6 Lower Mall, Hammersmith, London W 69 DS for £ 3.30 (1986).

16. *The Rowing Magazine*, published nine times a year features reports and articles on rowing in Great Britain and the world. It can be obtained for £ 7 a year (£ 11 overseas) from Ayling's Boathouse, Embankment, London SW 15 1LB.

IV. The History of Rowing: Most books on rowing in the 19th century began with brief histories of the sport. Even the books listed later in V. Style, Technique and Training, usually include some history. Histories of the sport at American universities and rowing clubs are still all too rare.

17. Rowe, R. P. P. and Pitman, C. M. *Rowing*. London: Longmans, 1898. The second edition of the first complete history of English rowing. ·

18. Cleaver, Hylton. *A History of Rowing*. London: Herbert Jenkins, 1957. Essentially this is a history of British rowing. The title is valid only to the extent that boat racing throughout the world had largely originated in England.

19. Gardner, John, "The Early Days of Rowing Sport," *The Log of the Mystic Seaport*, Vol. 19, No. 4, 114-123; reprinted in *The Log*, Vol. 32, No. 1, 3-9. A very useful description of early boat racing in America before 1860, with valuable details on the boats themselves by the Associate Curator of Small Craft at the Seaport.

20. Kelley, Robt. F. *American Rowing*. New York: G. P. Putnam, 1932. As rowing correspondent with the *New York Times* for almost 20 years Kelley learned much about the sport and wrote the only modern history. An excellent book in its journalistic way.

21. Burnell, Richard. *150 Years of the Oxford and Cambridge Boat Race.* Marlow, 1979. The most recent history of the oldest race for VIIIs in the world.

22. Burnell, Richard. *Henley Regatta.* London: O.U.P., 1957. A history of the regatta now over 140 years old which has attracted the best crews from all over the world.

23. Herrick, Robt. F. *Red Top.* Cambridge: Harvard U.P., 1948. These reminiscences of Harvard rowing are of more than local interest, but the inclusion of the most extensive bibliography on rowing by Fred Brittain makes *Red Top* invaluable.

24. Alma, Malcolm R. *Mark of the Oarsmen.* Syracuse: Syracuse Alumni Rowing Association, 1963. A narrative history of rowing at Syracuse since 1904.

25. Young, Charles Van P. *Courtney and Cornell Rowing.* Ithaca, Cornell Publications, 1923. While rather uncritical in his worship of the "Old Man," the author (a Cornell professor who knew Courtney) provides a very useful account of the emergence of the sport and development of a style.

26. *The H Book of Harvard Athletics*, Vol. I (1852-1922), John A. Blanchard, ed., Vol. II (1923-63), Geoffrey H. Movius, ed. Cambridge: Harvard Varsity Club, 1923, 1964. These histories have excellent sections on Harvard rowing for over a century.

27. *Sixty Years of the Union Boat Club* (1851-1911), by the Club Historian. Boston: The Union Boat Club, 1976. A useful account of the early days of rowing on the Charles.

28. Norsen, Irene W., *The Ward Brothers, Champions of the World.* New York: Vantage Press, 1958. Five of the sons of a Hudson River waterman became champion professional scullers and oarsmen. The youngest, Ellis, later coached at Pennsylvania from 1878 to 1913.

V. Style, Technique and Training: The debate over rowing styles will probably never end, if only because it is all too easy for the most efficient style to become stylized and lose its effectiveness. Training and conditioning a century ago were almost primitive by comparison with today when superior conditioning can often prove decisive. Again it seemed most useful to arrange the titles in order of publication which roughly reflects the sequence of styles.

29. Lehemann, R. C. *The Complete Oarsman.* London: Methuen, 1908. A classic which combines a history of boatracing, an exposition of the art and mystery of Orthodox oarsmanship and some reminiscences of "famous crews and memorable races." His *Selected Verse* (Edinburgh: Blackwood, 1929) puts him easily first among those who have celebrated the joy of rowing in verse.

30. Warre, Edmund. *On the Grammar of Rowing.* Oxford: Clarendon Press, 1909. Three short lectures by the great authority of English Orthodox style on how to teach the proper use of oar and slide to beginners.

31. Bourne, Gilbert C. *A Textbook on Oarsmanship.* Oxford: OUP, 1923. A thorough analysis of the stroke, oars, boats, coaching and the muscular action involved in rowing.

32. Cook, Theodore A. *Rowing at Henley.* Oxford: OUP, 1919. One of the historians of Henley races, Cook was also very interested in coaching for form and pace as well as in boats and their builders.

33. Glendon, Richard A. and Richard J. *Rowing.* New York: Lippincott, 1923. American oarsmen and coaches have not written much about rowing. So this book by the Glendons—father and son—self-taught American oarsmen and long-time coaches at the Naval Academy, provides a rare description of the Glendon stroke and the early years of American rowing.

34. Fairbairn, Steve. *On Rowing,* edited by Ian Fairbairn. London: Nicholas Kaye, 1951. Collected here are all three of Fairbairn's works on rowing.

35. Edwards, H. R. A. *The Way of a Man with a Blade.* London: Routledge and Kegan Paul, 1963. One of a half dozen or more books on rowing by English coaches. Edwards

was one of the first Englishmen to perceive the significance of Ratzeburg's ideas on technique, training and rig.

36. **Adam, Karl.** *Ratzeburg Rowing Clinic,* compiled and edited by University of Alabama Crew, 1970. A transcription of a rowing clinic conducted in the United States by Karl Adam and two colleagues. Coaching theory, technique, boats and rigging, physical and psychological training are all discussed.

37. **Wilson, Paul C.** *Modern Rowing.* Harrisburg, PA: Stackpole Co., 1969. A thorough analysis of Ratzeburg or International Modern style.

38. **Burnell, Richard.** *The Complete Sculler.* Marlow: Simpson, 1977. The last of Burnell's four books on sculling, with chapters on rigging, technique, training and sculling for rowing.

39. **Howard, Ronnie.** *Knowing Rowing.* Cranberry, N.J.: A. S. Barnes, 1977. An illustrated introduction to rowing and sculling.

40. **Astrand, P. O.** and **Rodahl, K.** *Textbook of Work Physiology.* New York: McGraw Hill, 1970. Assumes that sport is work and explains why and how! More specifically concerned with strength training for rowing are the three articles in *The Oarsman* by Timothy Michelson and Frederick C. Hagerman: "Training for Rowing," March–April, 1979, p. 12; May–June, 1979, pp. 6–10; Nov.-Dec., 1979, pp. 40-41.

41. Amateur Rowing Association, *Publications.* The British ARA has made available 16 pamphlets on various aspects of training for rowing. For the full list, write the ARA, (15) above. The catalogue of these publications can also be obtained from the Coaching Association of Canada, 333 River Road, Ottawa, Ontario, Canada K1L8B9.

Race Results

The selection of race results which follows is as modest as it is arbitrary. Some results are given because of their age and tradition. Others reflect something of the growth, depth and breadth of boat racing in America and of American rowers abroad. In general, match races between two or three colleges or boat clubs have not been included, although some of them, such as the Childs Cup Regatta between Pennsylvania, Princeton and Columbia which dates back to 1879, are truly venerable.

Although there is an attempt at consistency in presenting the results of a single series, no uniformity has been attempted for the results as a whole. Unfortunately, the reporting of boat races has never achieved anything like the scoring of a baseball game. With conditions of wind and water making a great difference, with a bewildering variety of distances to be raced and courses to be rowed on, comparative times cannot be pushed very far. Times have been given when available or when comparisons, as in the Olympics or World's, seemed useful.

To assemble even this arbitrary selection of race results has not been easy. Many books and people have helped along the way. The official results, for instance, of the Henley Royal Regatta are available in five books and now an annual publication with the year's results. Old programs, almanacs, NAAO *Rowing Guides*, *The Oarsman*, and newspaper files proved invaluable. The offices of Sports Information at Harvard, Yale and the University of Washington were most obliging. In particular, I thank Jack Franklin, Evelyn Bergman, W. Hart Perry and Peter Raymond from the NAAO; Clayton Chapman, Assistant to the Commissioner of EARC; Susan Urbas, Treasurer of the NWRA; Ted Hoag, Steve Gladstone, and David T. Swift. For all their help, many thanks. And they should bear no blame for any errors of omission or commission.

Harvard-Yale Race, 1852-1979

Though first rowed in 1852 at Lake Winnepesaukee, only in 1876 did the Harvard-Yale Race definitively become a two-boat race over a four mile straightaway. Two years later the race moved to New London where it has been held virtually every year since. Modeled on the Oxford-Cambridge race, the Harvard-Yale race is at present the only four-mile race left in the country, and American's oldest intercollegiate athletic event. Although the score stood even on five occasions (1901, 1911, 1915, 1922 and 1940) the recent string of Harvard victories has now put them ahead by 67 to 47.

Year	Date	Place	Miles	Direction	Winner	Harvard	Yale
1852	August 3	Winnepesaukee	2		Harvard	(by about 2 lengths) 22 min.[1]	24 min.[3]
1855	July 21	Springfield	3		Harvard	22 min. 47 sec.[2]	25 min.[4]
1859	July 26	Worcester	3[5]		Harvard	19 min. 18 sec.	20 min. 18 sec.
1860	July 24	Worcester	3		Harvard	18 min. 53 sec.	19 min. 5-1/2 sec.
1864	July 29	Worcester	3		Yale	19 min. 43-1/2 sec.	19 min. 1 sec.
1865	July 28	Worcester	3		Yale	19 min. 9 sec.	18 min. 42-1/2 sec.
1866	July 27	Worcester	3		Harvard	18 min. 43-1/4 sec.	19 min. 10 sec.
1867	July 19	Worcester	3		Harvard	18 min. 12-3/4 sec.	19 min. 25-1/2 sec.
1868	July 24	Worcester	3		Harvard	17 min. 48-1/2 sec.	18 min. 38-1/2 sec.
1869	July 23	Worcester	3		Harvard	18 min. 2 sec.	18 min. 11 sec.
1870	July 22	Worcester	3		Harvard	20 min. 30 sec.	(fouled)[6]
1872	July 24	Springfield	3[7]		Harvard	16 min. 57 sec.	18 min. 13 sec.
1873	July 17	Springfield	3		Yale	(uncertain)	16 min. 59 sec.
1874	July 18	Saratoga	3		Harvard	16 min. 56 sec.	(disabled)[8]
1875	July 14	Saratoga	3		Harvard	17 min. 5 sec.	17 min. 14-1/2 sec.
1876	June 30	Springfield	4[9]		Yale	22 min. 31 sec.	22 min. 2 sec.
1877	June 30	Springfield	4	Downstream	Harvard	24 min. 36 sec.	24 min. 43 sec.
1878	June 28	New London	4	Downstream	Harvard	20 min. 44-3/4 sec.	21 min. 29 sec.
1879	June 27	New London	4	Downstream	Harvard	22 min. 15 sec.	23 min. 58 sec.
1880	July 1	New London	4	Downstream	Yale	25 min. 9 sec.	24 min. 27 sec.
1881	July 1	New London	4	Downstream	Yale	22 min. 19 sec.	22 min. 13 sec.
1882	June 30	New London	4	Downstream	Harvard	20 min. 47-1/2 sec.	20 min. 50-1/2 sec.
1883	June 28	New London	4	Downstream	Harvard	25 min. 46-1/2 sec.	26 min. 59 sec.
1884	June 26	New London	4	Downstream	Yale	20 min. 48 sec.	20 min. 31 sec.
1885	June 26	New London	4	Downstream	Harvard	25 min. 15-1/2 sec.	26 min. 30 sec.
1886	July 2	New London	4	Upstream	Yale	21 min. 5 sec.	20 min. 42 sec.
1887	July 1	New London	4	Downstream	Yale	23 min. 10-1/2 sec.	22 min. 56 sec.
1888	June 29	New London	4	Downstream	Yale	21 min. 24 sec.	20 min. 10 sec.
1889	June 28	New London	4	Upstream	Yale	21 min. 55 sec.	21 min. 30 sec.
1890	June 27	New London	4	Downstream	Yale	21 min. 40 sec.	21 min. 29 sec.
1891	June 26	New London	4	Upstream	Harvard	21 min. 23 sec.	21 min. 57 sec.

Year	Month	Day	Location	No.	Direction	Winner	Time 1	Time 2
1892	July	1	New London	4	Downstream	Yale	21 min. 42-1/2 sec.	20 min. 48 sec.
1893	June	30	New London	4	Downstream	Yale	25 min. 15 sec.	25 min. 1-1/2 sec.
1894	June	28	New London	4	Downstream	Yale	24 min. 38 sec.	23 min. 45-1/2 sec.
1895	June	28	New London	4	Downstream	Yale	22 min. 5 sec.	21 min. 30 sec.
1897	June	25	Poughkeepsie	4[10]		Yale	21 min.	20 min. 44 sec.
1898	June	23	New London	4	Upstream	Yale	24 min. 35 sec.	24 min. 2 sec.
1899	June	29	New London	4	Downstream	Harvard	20 min. 52-1/2 sec.	21 min. 13 sec.
1900	June	28	New London	4	Downstream	Yale	21 min. 37-2/5 sec.	21 min. 12-4/5 sec.
1901	June	27	New London	4	Downstream	Yale	23 min. 45 sec.	23 min. 37 sec.
1902	June	26	New London	4	Downstream	Yale	20 min. 33 sec.	20 min. 20 sec.
1903	June	25	New London	4	Downstream	Yale	20 min. 29-3/5 sec.	20 min. 19-4/5 sec.
1904	July	1	New London	4	Upstream	Yale	22 min. 10 sec.	21 min. 40-1/2 sec.
1905	June	29	New London	4	Upstream	Yale	22 min. 36 sec.	22 min. 33-1/2 sec.
1906	June	28	New London	4	Downstream	Harvard	23 min. 2 sec.	23 min. 11 sec.
1907	June	27	New London	4	Upstream	Yale	21 min. 13 sec.	21 min. 10 sec.
1908	June	25	New London	4	Upstream	Harvard	24 min. 10 sec.	(not taken)[11]
1909	July	1	New London	4	Upstream	Harvard	21 min. 50 sec.	22 min. 10 sec.
1910	June	30	New London	4	Downstream	Harvard	20 min. 46-1/2 sec.	21 min. 4 sec.
1911	June	30	New London	4	Downstream	Harvard	22 min. 44 sec.	23 min. 40-1/2 sec.
1912	June	21	New London	4	Downstream	Harvard	21 min. 43-1/2 sec.	22 min. 4 sec.
1913	June	20	New London	4	Downstream	Harvard	21 min. 42 sec.	22 min. 20 sec.
1914	June	19	New London	4	Upstream	Yale	21 min. 16-1/5 sec.	21 min. 16 sec.
1915	June	25	New London	4	Upstream	Yale	21 min. 13-1/2 sec.	20 min. 52 sec.
1916	June	23	New London	4	Downstream	Harvard	20 min. 2 sec.	20 min. 17 sec.
1918	June	1	Derby, Conn.	2[12]		Harvard	10 min. 58 sec.	11 min. 4 sec.
1919	June	20	New London	4	Downstream	Yale	21 min. 47-3/5 sec.	21 min. 42-1/5 sec.
1920	June	25	New London	4	Upstream	Harvard	23 min. 11 sec.	23 min. 46 sec.
1921	June	24	New London	4	Downstream	Yale	20 min. 44-1/5 sec.	20 min. 41 sec.
1922	June	23	New London	4	Upstream	Yale	22 min. 6 sec.	21 min. 53 sec.
1923	June	22	New London	4	Downstream	Yale	22 min. 35 sec.	22 min. 10 sec.
1924	June	20	New London	4	Downstream	Yale	22 min. 11 sec.	21 min. 58-3/5 sec.
1925	June	19	New London	4	Upstream	Yale	20 min. 32-2/5 sec.	20 min. 26 sec.
1926	June	25	New London	4	Upstream	Yale	20 min. 21-3/5 sec.	20 min. 14-2/5 sec.

RACE RESULTS / 57

Year	Date	Place	Miles	Direction	Winner	Harvard	Yale
1927	June 24	New London	4	Downstream	Harvard	22 min. 35-1/5 sec.	22 min. 39 sec.
1928	June 22	New London	4	Downstream	Yale	20 min. 56 sec.	20 min. 21-3/5 sec.
1929	June 21	New London	4	Upstream	Yale	21 min. 39 sec.	21 min. 20 sec.
1930	June 20	New London	4	Downstream	Yale	20 min. 30-4/5 sec.	20 min. 9-2/5 sec.
1931	June 19	New London	4	Upstream	Harvard	22 min. 21 sec.	22 min. 30 sec.
1932	June 24	New London	4	Downstream	Harvard	21 min. 29 sec.	21 min. 42 sec.
1933	June 16	New London	4	Downstream	Harvard	22 min. 46-3/5 sec.	22 min. 53-3/5 sec.
1934	June 22	New London	4	Downstream	Yale	20 min. 1-3/5 sec.	19 min. 51-4/5 sec.
1935	June 22	New London	4	Upstream	Yale	21 min. 4 sec.	20 min. 19 sec.
1936	June 19	New London	4	Upstream	Harvard	20 min. 19 sec.	20 min. 40-3/5 sec.
1937	June 25	New London	4	Upstream	Harvard	20 min. 2 sec.	20 min. 6-2/5 sec.
1938	June 24	New London	4	Upstream	Harvard	20 min. 20 sec.	20 min. 23-4/5 sec.
1939	June 23	New London	4	Downstream	Harvard	20 min. 48-2/5 sec.	20 min. 53 sec.
1940	June 21	New London	4	Upstream	Harvard	21 min. 38 sec.	22 min. 9 sec.
1941	June 14	New London	4	Downstream	Harvard	20 min. 40 sec.	20 min. 53-2/5 sec.
1942	May 23	Derby, Conn.[13]	2		Harvard	10 min. 9-3/5 sec.	10 min. 20-4/5 sec.
1946	June 1	Boston[14]	1-3/4		Harvard	9 min. 18 sec.	9 min. 38 sec.
1947	June 18	New London	4	Upstream	Harvard	20 min. 40 sec.	20 min. 46 sec.
1948	June 25	New London	4	Downstream	Harvard	19 min. 21.4 sec.[15]	19 min. 23 sec.
1949	June 24	New London	4	Upstream	Yale	19 min. 54.2 sec.	19 min. 52.8 sec.
1950	June 23	New London	4	Downstream	Harvard	21 min. 36.4 sec.	21 min. 37.2 sec.
1951	June 22	New London	4	Downstream	Harvard	21 min. 26 sec.	21 min. 48.8 sec.
1952	June 20	New London	4	Upstream	Yale	22 min. 52.8 sec.	22 min. 49 sec.
1953	June 12	New London	4	Upstream	Harvard	20 min. 9 sec.	20 min. 20 sec.
1954	June 19	New London	4	Downstream	Yale	22 min. 2 sec.	21 min. 58.4 sec.
1955	June 17	New London	4	Upstream	Yale	20 min. 10 sec.	20 min. 5 sec.
1956	June 16	New London	4	Downstream	Yale	19 min. 47.4 sec.	19 min. 26 sec.
1957	June 15	New London	4	Upstream	Yale	21 min. 4 sec.	20 min. 35.2 sec.
1958	June 14	New London	4	Upstream	Yale	22 min. 52 sec.	22 min. 39 sec.
1959	June 13	New London	4	Downstream	Harvard	19 min. 52 sec.	20 min. 2 sec.
1960	June 18	New London	4	Downstream	Harvard	19 min. 41.2 sec.	20 min. 8.3 sec.

Year	Date	Location	No.	Direction	Winner	Time	Time
1961	June 17	New London	4	Downstream	Harvard	22 min. 00 sec.	22 min. 29.5 sec.
1962	June 16	New London	4	Upstream	Yale	21 min. 27 sec.	21 min. 26 sec.
1963	June 16	New London	4	Downstream	Harvard	19 min. 47 sec.	20 min. 15 sec.
1964	June 20	New London	4	Upstream	Harvard	20 min. 48.2 sec.	21 min. 6 sec.
1965	June 19	New London	4	Downstream	Harvard	19 min. 41.6 sec.	20 min. 21 sec.
1966	June 18	New London	4	Upstream	Harvard	19 min. 44 sec.	20 min. 06 sec.
1967	June 17	New London	4	Downstream	Harvard	22 min. 43.4 sec.	23 min. 08.2 sec.
1968	June 15	New London	4	Downstream	Harvard	20 min. 21 sec.	21 min. 05.4 sec.
1969	June 14	New London	4	Upstream	Harvard	19 min. 37.2 sec.	20 min. 09.2 sec.
1970	June 13	New London	4	Downstream	Harvard	22 min. 05 sec.	22 min. 34 sec.
1971	June 19	New London	4	Upstream	Harvard	22 min. 06 sec.	20 min. 52 sec.[17]
1972	June 17	New London	4	Downstream	Harvard	20 min. 43.3 sec.	20 min. 55.3 sec.
1973	June 16	New London	4	Downstream	Harvard	19 min. 52.8 sec.	20 min. 39.3 sec.
1974	May 18	Cambridge	3	Downstream	Harvard	16 min. 23.0 sec.	17 min. 34.0 sec.
1975	June 7	New London	4	Upstream	Harvard	22 min. 07 sec.	22 min. 49 sec.
1976	May 22	New London	4	Upstream	Harvard	23:43.9	24:47.9
1977	May 22	New London	2	Upstream	Harvard	9:42.6	9:57.7
1978	June 10	New London	4	Upstream	Harvard	23:26	23:39
1979	June 9	New London	4	Upstream	Harvard	19:22.9[16]	19:25.4

[1] "Iris," 8-oared, lapstreak boat with coxswain.
[2] "Y. Y." 4-oared, no rudder.
[3] "Nereid" 6-oared with coxswain.
[4] "Nautilus" 6-oared with coxswain.
[5] 1859–1879. Three miles with turn, 6-oared shells with rudder, steered by bow oar.
[6] Ran into Harvard, which was leading at the turning stake, Yale disqualified.
[7] 1872–1875. Intercollegiate Regattas. 3 miles straightaway.
[8] Collided with Harvard.
[9] Four miles straightaway. 8-oared shells, with coxswain.
[10] Triangular race. Harvard, Yale, Cornell, Cornell won.
[11] Yale stroke taken from shell near three mile mark.
[12] Two miles straightaway. 8-oared shells with coxswain.
[13] Two miles course, Housatonic River.
[14] Shortest Race of Series, Charles River.
[15] Downstream and Course Record.
[16] Upstream Record.
[17] Yale #7 lost oar, dove overboard at 2 mile mark.

National Association of Amateur Oarsmen:
National Championships, 1873-1979

In 1872 the amateur status of several oarsmen in the first extensive regatta for amateurs was loudly questioned. Later that year delegates from 30 clubs organized the NAAO and agreed on a definition of amateur which has prevailed virtually unchanged to this day.

The first National Championships were held in 1873 with races for Singles, Doubles and IVs without; Pairs without appeared the next year and in 1880 races for VIIIs were included. Since then events have been added, especially a set of races for 150 lb. crews and Intermediate as well as Senior or Elite races.

SENIOR SINGLE SCULLS
(Known as Association Senior Single Sculls 1873–1970)

(Distance, One Mile and One-Half)

1873—	Charles Meyers, Nassau B. C., New York City	10:08	1-4
1874—	F. E. Yates, New York A. C.	10:16	1-2
1875—	Charles E. Courtney, Union Springs (N.Y.) B. C.	9:46	
1876—	F. E. Yates, Union Springs	10:39	1-2
1877—	George W. Lee, Triton B.C., Newark N.J.	9:11	
1878—	George W. Lee, Triton B. C.	9:00	3-4
1879—	F. J. Mumford, Hope R. C., New Orleans, La.	9:50	
1880—	F. J. Mumford, Perservance B. C., New Orleans	10:05	3-4
1881—	F. E. Holmes, Pawtucket B. C.	9:06	3-4
1882—	F. E. Holmes, Pawtucket	10:05	
1883—	Joseph Laing, Grand Trunk B. C., Montreal, Canada	8:44	
1884—	Joseph Laing, Grand Trunk B. C.	9:28	1-2
1885—	Daniel J. Murphy, Crescent B. C., Boston, Mass.	9:42	
1886—	Martin F. Monahan, Albany R. C., Albany N.Y.	9:33	
1887—	J. F. Cobett, Farragut B. C., Chicago, Ill.	9:50	3-4
1888—	C. G. Psotta, Cornell University Navy	9:55	
1889—	D. Donohue, Nautilus R. C.	9:42	
1890—	William Caffrey, Lawrence C. C., Lawrence, Mass	10:18	1-4
1891—	William Caffrey, Lawrence C. C.	10:03	3-4
1892—	John J. Ryan, Sunnyside R. C., Toronto, Ont.	10:24	
1893X	John J. Ryan, Sunnyside R. C.	10:24	1-2
1894X	Ferdinand Koenig, Western R. C., St. Louis, Mo.	9:47	1-4
1895X	J. J. Whitehead, Riverside B. C.	10:00	
1896X	W. D. McDowell, Delaware B. C., Chicago, Ill.	9:50	
1897X	Joseph Maguire, Bradford B. C.	9:59	
1898X	E. H. TenEyck, Wachusett B. C.	9:59	

1899X	J. Rumohr, Rat Portage B. C., Rat Portage, Ont.	10:06	1-2
1900—	Frank B. Greer, Springfield B. C.	8:17	
1901X	C. S. Titus, Union B. C.	9:46	
1902X	James B. Juvenal, Vesper B. C., Philadelphia, Pa.	10:02	
1903X	L. F. Scholes, Toronto R. C.	9:56	1-4
1904X	D. B. Duffield, Detroit B. C.	10:08	3-4
1905X	Fred Sheppard, Seawanhaka B. C., Brooklyn, N.Y.	10:32	
1906X	Harry S. Bennett, Springfield B. C.	10:01	
1907—	Durando Miller, New York A. C.	9:04	2-5
1908—	John W. O'Neil, St. Mary's A. A. & A. C., Halifax, N. S.	10:17	
	(Distance changed to one mile and one-quarter)		
1909—	Wm. Mehrhof, Nassau B. C.	7:19	2-5
1910—	S. F. Gordon, Vesper B. C.	No Time Taken	
1911—	E. B. Butler, Argonaut R. C.	8:11	1-5
1912—	A. F. Culver, Winnipeg R. C.	7:26	
1913X	R. Dibble, Don Rowing Club	8:21	
1914—	John B. Kelly, Vesper B. C.	7:59	
1915X	Waldo Smith, New York A. C.	7:35	2-5
1916—	T. J. Rooney, Ravenswood B. C.	8:28	4-5
1917—No regatta held on account of World War.			
1918—No regatta held on account of World War.			
1919—	Paul Costello, Vesper Boat Club	7:39	
1920—	Louis Zoba, First Bohemian B. C., New York City	8:47	
1921—	Walter M. Hoover, Duluth B. C., Duluth, Minn.	7:45	1-5
1922—	Hilton Belyea, St. John Amateur R. C., Brunswick, N.S.	7:39	1-5
1923—	Edward McGuire, Mutual R. A., Buffalo, N.Y.	7:40	4-5
1924	W. E. Garrett Gilmore, Bachelors Barge Club Philadelphia Pa.	6:46	4-5
1925—	Russell Codman, Jr., Union B. C.	7:23	4-5
1926—	Robert H. Agnew, Undine Barge Club, Philadelphia, Pa.	7:17	3-5
1927—	Joe Wright, Jr., Argonaut R. C.	7:01	3-5
1928—	G. C. Turner, Penn A. C., Rowing Assn., Philadelphia, Pa.	7:48	
1929—	Kenneth Myers, Bachelors Barge Club	7:28	2-5
1930—	Leo B. Menne, Nassau Boat Club	9:26	
1931—	E. J. McGreal, Bachelors Barge Club	7:45	
1932—	Wesley E. Bevan, Undine Barge Club	8:11	
1933—	Albert B. Vogt, Penn A. C. Rowing Assn.	*5:20	
1934—	Winthrop Rutherfurd, Jr., Princeton University R. A.	†6:32	3-5
1935—	C. A. Campbell, Argonaut R. C.	7:34	2-5
1936—(Combined with Championship Single event.)			
1937—(Dropped from N.A.A.O. program)			
1938—	James Russell, Argonaut R. C.	8:19	3-5
1939—	Frank Silvio, New York A. C.	7:05	
1940—	Theo. A. Dubois, Winnipeg R. C., Winnipeg. Can.	7:45	4-5
1941—	Jos. Angyal, Ravenswood B. C.	10:05	2-5
1942—	Howard McCreech, Crescent B. C., Philadelphia, Pa.	7:42	
1943—	Arthur Gallagher, Penn A. C. Rowing Assn.	8:50	
1944—No regatta held on account of World War.			
1946—	John B. Kelly, Jr., Vesper Boat Club	No Time Taken	
1947—	Joseph McIntyre, Vesper Boat Club	7:13	

1948—	John S. Trinsey, Vesper Boat Club	8:17
1949—	Robert Williams, Leander B. C., Hamikon, Ont.	7:38.4
1950—	Jack Guest, Jr., Don R. C.	7:26
1951—	William Knecht, Vesper B. C.	7:59.3
1952—	Rudolph Jezek, New York A. C.	8:57.2
1953—	Walter Hoover, Jr., Detroit B. C.	7:36.4
	(Distance changed to 2000 meters)	
1954—	Pat Costello, Detroit Boat Club	8:05.3
1955—	Thomas McDonough, Fairmount R. A., Phil., Pa.	8:03.4
1956—	William Reimann, Undine Barge Club	7:17
1957—	Wm. Lang Jr., Minnesota B. C., St. Paul, Minn.	8:40.8
1958—	Paul Ignas, Vesper B. C.	7:29.2
1959—	Harry Parker, Vesper B. C.	7:52.5
1960—	Wayne Frye, Potamac B. C., Washington, D.C.	7:13.8
1961—	Seymour Cromwell, Riverside B. C.	7:15
1962—	Robert Lea III, Riverside B. C.	7:01
1963—	Donald M. Spero, Riverside B. C.	7:29.0
1964—	David Robinson, College B. C., Philadelphia, Pa.	7:21.3
1965—	William Maher, Detroit Boat Club	7:32.5
1966—	John Van Bloom, Long Beach R. A., Long Beach, Calif.	7:09
1967—	John Nunn, Long Beach R. A.	7:21.9
1968—	Thomas McKibbon, Long Beach R. A.	7:29.0
1969—	James Dietz, New York A. C.	8:22.0
1970—	Robert Gallagher, Fairmount, R. A.	7:43.4
1971—	James Castellan, Fairmount R. A.	7:57.5
1972—	Jody Trinsey, Malta B. C., Philadelphia, Pa.	8:46.1
1973—	P. Cortez, Vesper B. C.	7:55.0
1974—	Stout Long Beach	7:24.30
1975—	Guy Iverson, Undine B. C.	7:56.66
1976—	Eric Meyers, Potomac	7:18.9
1977—	Ted Van Dusen, Riverside	8:18.5
1978—	T. Hazeltine, Undine B	7:16.2
1979—	Gary Wojilyla Detroit B. C.	7:18.06

X-Race Rowed with one turn †Distance, 1 Mile *Distance 1/4 Mile ¶Distance, 2000 Meters

ELITE SINGLE SCULLS
(Known as Senior Single Sculls 1899–1970)

(Distance, One Mile and One-Half)

1899X	E. Hanlan TenEyck, Wachusett B. C.	10:16	1-4
1900—	John Rumohr, Harlem R. C., New York City (RO)	10:52	1-2
1901X	E. Hanlan TenEyck, Wachusett B. C.	9:54	1-2
1902X	C. S. Titus, Union B. C., N. Y. C.	9:59	1-2
1903X	Frank B. Greer, East Boston A. A., Boston Mass.	9:38	3-4
1904X	Frank B. Greer, East Boston A. A.	10:08	1-2
1905X	Frank B. Greer, East Boston A. A.	9:47	1-5

1906X	C. S. Titus, Nonpareil R. C., New York City	10:05
1907—	Harry S. Bennett, Springfield B. C.	9:08 3-5
1908—	Frank B. Greer, East Boston A. A.	9:53
	(Distance changed to one mile and one-quarter)	
1909—	John W. O'Neil, St. Mary's A. A. & A. C.	7:19 2-5
1910—	William Mehrhof, Nassau B. C., New York City	8:34
1911—	E. B. Butler, Argonaut R. C.	7:56 3-5
1912—	E. B. Butler, Argonaut R. C.	8:22 2-5
1913X	R. Dibble, Don R. C.	8:19
1914—	R. Dibble, Don R. C.	7:48
1915X	R. Dibble, Don R. C.	7:27 3-5
1916—	T. J. Rooney, Ravenswood B. C.	9:06 2-5
1917—No regatta held on account of World War.		
1918—No regatta held on account of World War.		
1919—	John B. Kelly, Vesper B. C.	7:51
1920—	John B. Kelly, Vesper B. C.	7:57
1921—	Walter M. Hoover, Duluth B. C.	
1922—	Paul V. Costello, Vesper B. C.	7:27 1-5
1923—	Edward McGuire, Mutual R. C.	8:48
1924—	W. E. Garrett Gilmore, Bachelors Barge Club	Row Over
1925—	Walter M. Hoover, Undine Barge Club	7:46 3-5
1926—	Walter M. Hoover, Undine Barge Club	7:33 3-5
1927—	Jos. Wright, Jr., Argonaut R. C.	7:18
1928—	G. Chester Turner, Penn A. C., Rowing Assn.	8:00
1929—	Kenneth Myers, Bachelors Barge Club	8:18 4-5
1930—	Wm. G. Miller, Bachelors Barge Club	7:56 4-5
1931—	Wm. G. Miller, Bachelors Barge Club	7:03 2-5
1932—	Wm. G. Miller, Penn A. C. Rowing Assn.	8:07
1933—	Wm. G. Miller, Penn A. C. Rowing Assn.	*5:21
1934—	Winthrop Rutherford, Jr., Princeton University R. A.	†6:23
1935—	C. A. Campbell, Argonaut R. C.	7:35
1936—	Dan H. Barrow, Jr., Penn A. C. Rowing Assn.	7:36 2-5
1937—	Jos. W. Burk, Penn A. C. Rowing Assn.	7:00 1-5
1938—	Jos. W. Burk, Penn A. C. Rowing Assn	Row Over
1939—	Jos. W. Burk, Penn A. C. Rowing Assn.	7:20
1940—	Jos. W. Burk, Penn A. C. Rowing Assn.	7:51 2-5
1941—	Theo A. DuBois, Winnipeg R. C.	8:35 1-5
1942—	Jos. Angyal, Ravenswood B. C.	7:55 1-5
1943—	A. Gallagher, Penn A. C. Rowing Assn.	Row Over
1944-1945—No regatta held on account of World War.		
1946—	John B. Kelly, Jr., Vesper Boat Club	8:15 2-5
1947—	Theo A. DuBois, Winnipeg R. C.	7:28 4-5
1948—	John B. Kelly, Jr., Vesper Boat Club	7:20.9
1949—	Joseph Angyal, New York A. C.	7:20
1950—	John B. Kelly, Jr., Vesper B. C.	7:39
1951—	Robert Williams, Leander, B. C.	8:35.2
1952—	John B. Kelly, Jr., U.S. Navy	7:21.8
1953—	John B. Kelly, Jr., Vesper Boat Club	7:54
	(Distance changed to 2000 meters)	
1954—	John B. Kelly, Jr., Vesper Boat Club	8:45.8

1955—	John B. Kelly, Jr., Vesper Boat Club	7:39
1956—	John B. Kelly, Jr., Vesper Boat Club	8:15.3
1957—	Thomas McDonough, Fairmount R. A.	8:07.6
1958—	Paul Ignas, Vesper Boat Club	7:20.6
1959—	Harry Parker, Vesper Boat Club	7:12.8
1960—	Harry Parker, Vesper Boat Club	8:25.2
1961—	Seymour Cromwell, Riverside, B. C., Boston, Mass.	Row Over
1962—	Seymour Cromwell, Riverside B. C.	7:02.2
1963—	Donald M. Spero, Riverside B. C.	7:12.0
1964—	Donald M. Spero, New York A. C.	7:42.2
1965—	William Maher, Detroit Boat Club	8:10
1966—	Donald M. Spero, New York, A. C.	7:39.2
1967—	William Maher, Detroit Boat Club	6:50
1968—	Thomas McKibbon, Long Beach R. A.	7:22.7
1969—	Wm. Maher, Vesper—U.S. Army	8:02.1
1970—	James W. Dietz, New York A. C.	6:50.4
1971—	James W. Dietz, New York A. C.	7:14
1972—	James W. Dietz, New York A. C.	8:08.7
1973—	James W. Dietz, N.Y. A. C.	7:08.7
1974—	Sean Drea, Undine B. C.	8:08.97
1975—	Sean Drea, Undine B. C.	7:38.25
1976—	Sean Drea, Undine B. C.	7:12
1977—	Sean Drea, Undine B. C.	6:5.85
1978—	J. Dietz, New York A. C.	7:01.6
1979—	Gregg Stone, Harvard U	7:27.28

X-Race Rowed with one turn †Distance, 1 Mile *Distance, 1/4 Mile ¶Distance, 2000 Meters

ELITE DOUBLE SCULLS
(Known as Senior Double Sculls 1873–1970)

(Distance, One Mile and One-Half)

1873—	Steel and Witmer, Crescent B. C.	9:30	
1874—	Yates and Curtis, New York A. C.	9:37	1-4
1875—	Robinson and Courtney, Union Springs B. C.	8:50	1-2
1876—	Robinson and Courtney, Union Springs B. C.	9:19	
1877—	McBeath and Henderson, Quaker City B. C.	8:18	
1878—	O'Donnel and Powers, Hope R. C.	8:37	1-4
1879—	Rathbone and Lyon, New York A. C.	9:18	3-4
1880—	Whitaker and Holmes, Pawtucket B. C.	9:41	
1881—	Appley and Holmes, Pawtucket B. C., Maine	8:37	1-2
1882—	O'Connell and Buckley, Portland B. C.	9:30	
1883—	O'Connell and Buckley, Portland B. C.	8:16	
1884—	Enright and O'Connor, Toronto R. C.	9:07	1-2
1885—	Monahan Bros., Albany R. C. (RO)	No Time Taken	
1886—	Korf and Winand, Delaware B. C.	9:18	1-4

1887—	John O. Regan, stroke; Wm. Goeffert, bow; Metropolitan R. C.	10:19
1888—	Don Amateur R. C.	9:20
1889—	Pilkington and Nagle, Metropolitan R. C.	8:45
1890—	Bayside R. C. Toronto, Ont.	9:14
1891—	E. J. Mulcahy and M. F. Monahan, Albany	8:39
1892—	Vesper Boat Club	9:53 1-4
1893X	Van Vleet and Megowan, Vesper B. C.	9:50
1894X	Van Vleet and Baltz, Vesper B. C.	9:06 1-2
1895X	Hawkins and Nagle, Harlem R. C.	8:43
1896X	Crawford and Howard, New York A. C.	9:10 3-4
1897X	Van Vleet and Monaghan, Penn. Barge Club, Phila., Pa.	9:27 3-4
1898X	Edward Hanlan TenEyck and C. H. Lewis, Wachusett BC	9:09
1899X	Edward Hanlan TenEyck and C. H. Lewis, Wachusett BC	9:19 3-4
1900—	Edward Hanlan TenEyck and C. H. Lewis, Wachusett B. C.	Row Over No Time Taken
1901X	Edward Hanlan TenEyck and C. H. Lewis, Wachusett B. C.	8:59
1902X	Frank Vesely, bow; Fred Budric, stroke: First Bohemian B. C.	9:34
1903X	L. F. Scholes, bow; F. S. Smith, stroke; Toronto B. C.	9:14
1904X	John F. Mulcahy, bow; Wm. M. Varley, stroke; Atlanta B. C., New York City	10:03 1-4
1905X	C. S. Titus, bow; C. Steinkamp, stroke; Nonpareil R. C.	10:29
1906X	F. W. Swallow, bow; P. N. Kirk, stroke; Crescent B. C.	9:25
1907—	H. Jacob, bow; W. Bowler, stroke; Don Rowing Club	8:18 1-5
1908—	H. Bennett, bow; A. Warnock, stroke; Springfield B. C. (Distance changed to one mile and one-quarter)	9:28 1-5
1909—	F. Fuessel, bow; F. Shepherd, stroke, Harlem R. C.	6:53
1910—	Fred Fuessel, bow; Fred Shepherd, stroke; Harlem R. C.	No Time Taken
1911—	George W. Engle and Samuel F. Gordon, Vesper B. C.	7:31
1912—	A. F. Culver and F. F. Carruthers, Winnipeg	7:57
1913—	R. Dibble and R. H. Lepper, Don R. C.	7:45 2-5
1914—	Walter L. Smith and John B. Kelly, Vesper B. C.	7:45
1915X	W. M. Hoover and A. R. Kent, Duluth B. C.	7:05
1916—	A. J. Osman and A. R. Kent, Duluth B. C.	7:05
1919—	Riverside Boat Club	7:45
1920—	Vesper Boat Club	7:44
1921—	Vesper Boat Club	Row Over
1922—	Bachelors Barge Club	7:05
1923—	Penn A. C. Rowing Assn.	7:16 1-5
1924—	Undine Barge Club	6:39 2-5
1925—	Malta Boat Club	7:19
1926—	Undine Barge Club	7:07
1927—	Bachelors Barge Club	6:09
1928—	Bachelors Barge Club	7:10
1929—	Undine Barge Club	Row Over
1930—	Bachelors Barge Club	8:17 3-5
1931—	Bachelors Barge Club	7:28
1932—	Bachelors Barge Club	7:29
1933—	Penn A. C. Rowing Assn.	*4:37 3-5

1934—	Penn A. C. Rowing Assn.	†6:03 2-5
1935—	Penn A. C. Rowing Assn.	7:09 2-5
1936—	Undine Barge Club	¶7:50
1937—	Undine Barge Club	6:55
1938—	Bachelors Barge Club	7:27 4-5
1939—	Winnipeg Rowing Club	6:58 2-5
1940—	Penn A. C. Rowing Assn.	7:51 1-5
1941—	Worchester R. C.	7:52 3-5
1942—	Fairmount Rowing Association	7:27
1943—	Penn A. C. Rowing Association	No Time Taken
1944-1945—No regatta held on account of World War.		
1946—	Vesper Boat Club	7:10
1947—	Ottawa Rowing Club, Ottawa, Can.	6:39 3-5
1948—	Art Gallagher, Penn A. C. Rowing Assn., John Angyal,	
	New York A. C. Combination Crew	¶6:56
1949—	Malta Boat Club	6:47.4
1950—	Vesper Boat Club	7:06 3-5
1951—	Vesper Boat Club	7:43.3
1952—	Detroit Boat Club	6:51.4
1953—	Vesper Boat Club	7:31.4
	(Distance changed to 2000 meters)	
1954—	Detroit Boat Club	8:10.4
1955—	Detroit Boat Club	7:30.5
1956—	Detroit Boat Club	7:46.4
1957—	Minnesota B. C.	7:32.2
1958—	Detroit Boat Club	No Time Taken
1959—	Vesper Boat Club	7:25.5
1960—	John B. Kelly, Jr. and Wm. Knecht, Vesper B. C.	8:00.3
1961—	William Flint and Ted Nash, Lake Washington R. C.	
	Seattle, Washington	6:35.1
1962—	Wm. Knecht and Dave Wilmerding, Vesper B. C.	6:57.8
1963—	Donald Spero and Seymour Cromwell, Riverside B. C.	6:33.0
1964—	Robert C. Lea, III, and Richard Keyes, Vesper B. C.	6:56.3
1965—	David Robinson and Al Wachlin, Fairmount R. A.	7:02.4
1966—	Seymour Cromwell and James Storm, San Diego R. C.,	
	San Diego, Calif.	6:43.5
1967—	John Nunn and John Van Bloom, Long Beach R. A.	7:33.2
1968—	Paul Wilson and Robert Arlett, Vesper B. C.	6:38.0
1969—	Thomas McKibbon and John Van Bloom, Long Beach	
	R. A.	
1970—	Thomas McKibbon and John Van Bloom, Long Beach	
	R. A.	No Time taken
1971—	New York A. C.	7:02
1972—	Long Beach R. A.	6:45.4
1973—	NYAC	6:58.9
1974—	NYAC	6:48.19
1975—	NYAC (Klecatsky, Dietz)	7:11.66
1976—	NYAC (Klecatsky, Dietz)	6:57.6
1977—	Malta (Depman, Sutter)	7:36.8
1978—	Harvard (Wood, Stone)	6:34.6

1979—   NYAC (Belden, Dietz)   6:26.50

X-Race Rowed with one turn †Distance 1 Mile *Distance, 1/4 Mile ¶ Distance, 2000
Meters

ELITE PAIR—OARED SHELLS WITHOUT COXSWAIN
(Known as Senior Pair—Oared w/o Coxswain 1874-1970)

(Distance, One Mile and One-Half)

1874—	Argonauta Rowing Assn., Bergen Point, N.J.		9:41	1-2
1875—	Argonauta Rowing Assn.		9:30	
1876—	Atalanta Boat Club		10:10	3-4
1877—	Emerald Boat Club, Detroit, Michigan		9:04	
1878—	Mutual Boat Club		8:56	3-4
1879—	Olympic Boat Club, Albany, N.Y.		9:41	3-4
1880—	Mutual Boat Club		10:07	1-2
1881—	Detroit Boat Club		9:33	
1882—	Mutual Boat Club		10:38	
1883—	Mutual Boat Club		8:54	
1884—	Mutual Boat Club	(Row Over)	9:24	
1885—	Ariel Boat Club, Newark, N.J.		9:33	
1886—	Eureka Boat Club, Newark, N.J.		9:33	1-4
1887—	Modoc Rowing Club, St. Louis, Mo.		10:00	3-4
1888—	Seawanhaka Boat Club	(Row Over)	18:13	
1889—	Garfield Beach Boat Club, Salt Lake City, Utah		9:18	
1890—	Detroit Boat Club		10:15	1-4
1891—	Atalanta Boat Club		10:12	3-4
1892—	Atalanta Boat Club		10:14	3-4
1893—	Detroit Boat Club		10:05	
1894—	Vesper Boat Club		10:24	
1895—	Toronto Rowing Club		9:46	
1896—	Pennsylvania Boat Club		10:05	1-4
1897—	Argonaut Rowing Club		10:17	
1898—	Pennsylvania Boat Club		9:59	
1899—	Pennsylvania Boat Club		10:33	1-4
1900—	Vesper Boat Club		9:33	1-2
1901—	Vesper Boat Club		9:44	
1902—	Vesper Boat Club		11:02	
1903—	Harlem Rowing Club		11:09	1-4
1904—	Seawanhaka Boat Club		10:57	
1905—	Seawanhaka Boat Club		10:19	
1906—	Metropolitan Rowing Club		10:50	
1907—	Argonaut Rowing Club		9:16	1-5
1908—	Vesper Boat Club		10:00	
1932—	Undine Barge Club		¶8:31	3-5
1936—	Penn A. C. Rowing Club		7:50	
1946—	Fairmount Rowing Assn.		7:56	3-5
1947—	West Side Rowing Club		6:55	

1948—	Yale University R. A., New Haven, Conn.	¶7:20.7
1949—	Fairmount Rowing Assn.	7:08.8
1950—	Fairmount Rowing Assn.	7:24 2-5
1951—	Fairmount Rowing Assn.	8:33.1
1952—	Rutgers University, New Brunswick, N.J.	7:08.2
1953—	West Side Rowing Club	8:06.4
	(Distance changed to 2000 meters)	
1954—	Rutgers Rowing Club	8:28.2
1955—	New York Athletic Club	7:45
1956—	U.S. Navy, Annapolis, Maryland	7:22.8
1957—	Washington A. C., Seattle, Washington	7:46
1958—	Washington A. C.	7:09
1959—	Lake Washington Rowing Club	7:27.8
1960—	Lake Washington Rowing Club	7:47.2
1961—	Stanford Crew Association, Palo Alto, Calif.	6:58.3
1962—	Lake Washington Rowing Club	7:09.4
1963—	Potomac B. C.	7:18.3
1964—	Vesper Boat Club	7:23.4
1965—	Vesper Boat Club	7:38.6
1966—	Union Boat Club	7:22
1967—	Potomac B. C.	6:36.6
1968—	Potomac B. C.	6:57.2
1969—	Potomac B. C.	7:07.2
1970—	Union Boat Club	7:23
1971—	Union Boat Club	7:14.5
1972—	Stanford C. A., Palo Alto., Calif.	7:36.1
1973—	Vesper Boat Club	7:03.6
1974—	Vesper Boat Club	7:52.44
1975—	Vesper Boat Club (Miller, Moroney)	7:29.83
1976—	Potomac Boat Club (Blakeley, Borchelt)	7:12.0
1977—	College B. C. (Ibbotson, Watchpaugh)	6:47.5
1978—	U. Penn (Colgan, Ibbotson)	6:49
1979—	Harvard A (Fellows, Cashin)	7:07.8

ELITE PAIR—OARED SHELLS WITH COXSWAIN
(Known as Senior Pair—Oared with Coxswain 1932-1970)

1932—	Pennsylvania Barge Club	¶8:43
1946—	Vesper Boat Club	9:31
1947—	Vesper Boat Club	8:30
1948—	Vesper Boat Club	7:22.3
1949—	Fairmount Rowing Assn.	8:41.8
1950—	Fairmount Rowing Assn.	7:42
1951—	New York Athletic Club	8:51.7
1952—	Stanford University	7:39.6
1953—	Detroit Boat Club	7:49.8
	(Distance changed to 2000 meters)	
1954—	Fairmount Rowing Assn.	7:38.8

1955—	Fairmount Rowing Assn.	8:40
1956—	Stanford Crew Assn.	8:46.3
1957—	Washington A. C.	8:25
1958—	Vesper Boat Club	7:58.2
1959—	Detroit Boat Club	7:27.2
1960—	Lake Washington Rowing Club	8:37.7
1961—	Stanford Crew Assn.	7:47
1962—	Stanford Crew Assn.	7:21.3
1963—	Vesper Boat Club	7:45.4
1964—	Vesper Boat Club	7:19.8
1965—	Vesper Boat Club	7:43
1966—	Vesper Boat Club	7:19.7
1967—	Potomac B. C.	7:14.8
1968—	Potomac B. C.	7:27.2
1969—	Potomac B. C.	7:58.9
1970—	Union B. C.	7:22.4
1971—	Long Beach R. A.	7:34
1972—	College B. C.	7:25.4
1973—	Vesper Boat Club	7:51.8
1974—	Vesper/Union	7:33.1
1975—	Vesper (Matthews, Vreugdenhil, Dreyfuss)	7:47.33
1976—	Vesper (Matthews, Vreugdenhil, Dreyfuss)	7:43.8
1977—	College B. C. (Watchpaugh, Ibbotson, Chatsky)	8:30.0
1978—	U. of Penn (Woodman, Stebl, Chatsky)	7:14.8
1979—	U. of Penn (Woodman, Stebl, Chatsky)	7:13.59

Rev. 1977

ELITE FOUR—OARED SHELLS WITHOUT COXSWAIN
(Known as Senior Four-Oared w/o Cox 1873–1970)

(Distance, One Mile and One-Half)

1873—	Argonauta Rowing Assn.	8:16	
1874—	Beaverwyck Rowing Club, Albany, N.Y.	8:45	1-2
1875—	Atalanta Boat Club	8:34	1-4
1876—	Atalanta Boat Club	9:36	3-4
1877—	Emerald Boat Club	7:50	
1878—	Mutual Boat Club	8:04	
1879—	Hillsdale Rowing Club, Hillsdale, Mich.	8:23	3-4
1880—	Hillsdale Rowing Club	8:53	
1881—	Hillsdale Rowing Club	8:06	1-2
1882—	Centenial Boat Club, Detroit, Mich.	8:27	
1883—	Eureka Boat Club	8:16	1-4
1884—	Argonaut Rowing Club	8:22	3-4
1885—	Nautilus Rowing Club	8:23	
1886—	Fairmount Rowing Assn.	8:01	1-4
1887—	Toronto Rowing Club	9:15	
1888—	Passaic Boat Club, Newark, N.J.	8:47	1-4
1889—	Winnipeg Rowing Club	8:42	

1890—	Bradford Boat Club	8:40 3-4
1891—	Fairmount Rowing Assn.	8:54 1-2
1892—	Wyandotte Boat Club	9:00
1893X	Minnesota Boat Club	9:13
1894X	Argonaut Rowing Club	8:48
1895X	Institute Boat Club, Newark, N.J.	8:43 1-2
1896X	Winnipeg Rowing Club	8:59 1-2
1897X	Institute Boat Club	9:07
1898X	Argonaut Rowing Club	9:02
1899X	Pennsylvania Barge Club	8:48 1-4
1900—	Detroit Boat Club	9:18
1901X	Western Rowing Club	9:09
1902X	Winnipeg Rowing Club	8:55 1-4
1903X	Winnipeg Rowing Club	9:04
1904X	Century Boat Club	9:05 1-4
1905X	Seawanhaka Boat Club	9:53 2-5
1906X	Winnipeg Rowing Club	No Time Taken
1907—	Argonaut Rowing Club	8:10 1-5
1908—	Vesper Boat Club	8:58 1-2

(Distance Changed to one mile and one-quarter)

1909—	Ottawa Rowing Club	6:29
1910—	Arundel Boat Club, Baltimore, Md.	7:04 3-5
1911—	Argonaut Rowing Club	7:05
1912—	Winnipeg Rowing Club	7:22
1913X	Duluth Boat Club	7:34
1914—	University Barge Club	7:12
1915X	Duluth Boat Club	6:52 4-5
1916—	Duluth Boat Club	7:49 2-5

1917—No Regatta held on account of World War.
1918—No Regatta held on account of World War.

1919—	Century Boat Club	6:05 2-5
1920—	Pennsylvania Barge Club	7:14
1921—	Vesper Boat Club	
1922—	Duluth Boat Club	7:00
1923—	Pennsylvania Barge Club	7:25
1924—	West Philadelphia Boat Club, Philadelphia, Pa.	6:25
1925—	No race	
1926—	Bachelors Barge Club	6:42 3-5
1927—	Pennsylvania Barge Club	6:25 3-5
1928—	Bachelors Barge Club	7:18
1929—	South Side Boat Club, Quincy, Ill.	7:43 3-5
1930—	Bachelors Barge Club	8:01
1931—	Bachelors Barge Club	6:45
1932—	Penn A. C. Rowing Assn.	7:37
1933—	Bachelors Barge Club	*4:29
1934—	Penn A. C. Rowing Assn	†Row Over
1935—	Bachelors Barge Club	7:01
1936—	West Side Rowing Club	¶7:07
1937—	West Side Rowing Club	6:41 4-5
1938—	West Side Rowing Club	7:34

1939—	West Side Rowing Club	6:40 3-5
1940—	Detroit Boat Club	7:22
1941—	Fairmount Rowing Assn.	8:31 2-5
1942—	Fairmount Rowing Assn.	6:53 3-5
1943—	Fairmount Rowing Assn.	No Time Taken
1944-1945—No Regatta held on account of World War.		
1946—	Detroit Boat Club	8:30 3-5
1947—	Vesper Boat Club	6:23
1948—	Yale University	¶6:40.5
1949—	Vesper Boat Club	6:34
1950—	Vesper Boat Club	6:43 2-5
1951—	Detroit Boat Club	7:21.8
1952—	H. S. Naval Academy, Annapolis, Md.	6:34.1
1953—	West Side Rowing Club	6:43
	(Distance changed to 2000 meters)	
1954—	West Side Rowing Club	7:14.2
1955—	West Side Rowing Club	6:57
1956—	Detroit Boat Club	7:13
1957—	Washington A. C.	7:08
1958—	West Side Rowing Club	6:41.2
1959—	Lake Washington Rowing Club	6:18.4
1960—	Lake Washington Rowing Club	7:16.0
1961—	Lake Washington Rowing Club	6:28.3
1962—	Lake Washington Rowing Club	6:20.4
1963—	Lake Washington Rowing Club	6:30.0
1964—	St. Catharines Rowing Club, St. Catharines, Ont.	6:41.2
1965—	Vesper Boat Club	6:40.2
1966—	Stanford Crew Assn.	6:39
1967—	Vesper Boat Club, Pa.	6:37.9
1968—	Vesper Boat Club	6:29.0
1969—	Vesper Boat Club	6:45
1970—	Vesper Boat Club	6:18.6
1971—	Vesper B. C.	6:44
1972—	Vesper B. C.	6:22.9
1973—	Vesper	6:37.2
1974—	Vesper/NYAC	6:25.2
1975—	Vesper	6:37.17
1976—	Vesper	7:16.0-Row Over
1977—	Potomac	6:49.0
1978—	Cornell/Potomac	6:15
1979—	U. of Penn.	6:14.16

Rev. 1977

ELITE FOUR—OARED SHELLS WITH COXSWAIN
(Known as Senior Four-Oared with Cox 1928-1970)

(Distance, One Mile and One-Quarter)

1928—	Bachelors Barge Club	7:49 3-5
1929—	Penn A. C. Rowing Assn.	Row Over

1930—	Bachelors Barge Club	8:05	4-5
1931—	Bachelors Barge Club	7:13	3-5
1932—	Penn A. C. Rowing Assn.	7:44	
1933—	South End Rowing Club, San Francisco, Calif.	*4:49	
1934—	Penn A. C. Rowing Assn.	†6:02	
1935—	West Side Rowing Club	7:15	3-5
1936—	Riverside Boat Club	¶6:58	3-5
1937—	West Side Rowing Club	Row Over	
1938—	West Side Rowing Club	7:33	3-5
1939—	Penn A. C. Rowing Assn.	6:18	
1940—	Penn A. C. Rowing Assn.	7:04	4-5
1941—	West Side Rowing Club	9:00	2-5
1942—	Fairmount Rowing Assn.	7:05	1-5
1943—	Wyandotte Boat Club	7:54	
1944-1945—No regatta held on account of World War.			
1946—	Detroit Boat Club	8:03	3-5
1947—	West Side Rowing Club	6:40	
1948—	University of Washington, Seattle, Washington	¶6:43.3	
1949—	West Side Rowing Club	6:44.4	
1950—	West Side Rowing Club	7:01	
1951—	West Side Rowing Club	7:40	
1952—	University of Washington	6:46	
1953—	Detroit Boat Club	7:03.8	
(Distance changed to 2000 meters)			
1954—	Vesper Boat Club	6:54.5	
1955—	West Side Rowing Club	7:25	
1956—	West Side Rowing Club	7:13.8	
1957—	Detroit Boat Club	7:19.4	
1958—	Vesper Boat Club	6:42.4	
1959—	Lake Washington Rowing Club	6:24.2	
1960—	Lake Washington Rowing Club	7:12.6	
1961—	Lake Washington Rowing Club	7:07.8	
1962—	Lake Washington Rowing Club	6:34.4	
1963—	Riverside B. C.	6:43.8	
1964—	Harvard University, Cambridge, Mass.	6:33.1	
1965—	Vesper Boat Club	6:46.2	
1966—	St. Catharines Rowing Club	6:31.3	
1967—	New Zealand R. A., New Zealand	6:32	
1968—	Vesper Boat Club	6:34.6	
1969—	Union Boat Club	7:19.9	
1970—	New Zealand R. A.	6:37.2	
1971—	Vesper B. C.		
1972—	Univ. of PA		
1973—	Vesper B. C.	6:39.8	
1974—	N. A. A. O. Camp	6:54.97	
1975—	Vesper B. C.	6:45.81	
1976—	Vesper B. C.	6:50.5	
1977—	U. of Penn.	6:26.7	
1978—	U. of Penn.	6:32.2	
1979—	Harvard	7:00.15	

*Distance, 3/4 mile. †Distance, 1 mile. ¶Distance, 2000 meters.

ELITE EIGHT—OARED SHELLS
(Known as Senior Eight Shells 1880–1970)

(Distance, One Mile and One-Half)

1880—	Dauntless Rowing Club	8:55	
1881—	Narragansett Boat Club, Providence, RI	7:51	1-4
1882—			
1883—	Metropolitan R. C.	7:51	
1884—	Columbia A. C., Washington, D. C. (RO)	8:23	
1885—	Columbia A. C.	7:46	3-4
1886—	Fairmount Rowing Assn.	8:47	
1887—	Vesper Boat Club	8:23	1-2
1888—	Fairmount Rowing Assn.	8:32	1-2
1889—	Atalanta Boat Club	7:41	
1890—	Atalanta Boat Club	8:12	3-4
1891—	New York A. C.	7:47	1-2
1892—	New York A. C.	7:55	
1893—	Atalanta Boat Club	7:55	1-2
1894—	Triton Boat Club	7:36	1-2
1895—	First Bohemian Boat Club	7:39	1-2
1896—	Baltimore A. C., Baltimore, Md.	7:48	
1897—	Pennsylvania Barge Club	8:01	1-4
1898—	Pennsylvania Barge Club	7:40	1-2
1899—	Pennsylvania Barge Club	7:40	1-2
1900—	Vesper Boat Club	9:01	1-4
1901—	Argonaut Boat Club	7:49	
1902—	Vesper Boat Club	7:57	1-4
1903—	Winnipeg Rowing Club	7:52	
1904—	Vesper Boat Club	7:50	
1905—	Argonaut Rowing Club	7:22	1-5
1906—	Dead heat between New York A. C. and Riverside B. C.	No Time Taken	
1907—	Argonaut Rowing Club	7:35	
1908—	New York A. C.	8:44	

(Distance changed to one mile and one-quarter)

1909—	New York A. C.	6:05	
1910—	Ottawa Rowing Club	6:33	3-5
1911—	Argonaut Rowing Club	6:11	1-5
1912—	Winnipeg Rowing Club	6:37	
1913—	Duluth Boat Club	6:58	
1914—	Duluth Boat Club	6:27	2-5
1915—	Duluth Boat Club	5:30	3-5
1916—	Duluth Boat Club	7:13	1-5
1917—No regatta held on account of World War.			
1918—No regatta held on account of World War.			
1919—	Duluth Boat Club		
1920—	Navy Athletic Assn.	6:20	
1921—	Duluth Boat Club		
1922—	Duluth Boat Club	6:20	
1923—	Undine Barge Club	6:35	1-5
1924—	New York A. C.	5:55	3-5
1925—	Pennsylvania Barge Club	6:33	2-5

1926—	Penn A. C. Rowing Assn.	6:23 2-5
1927—	Wyandotte Boat Club, Wyandotte, Mich.	6:19 1-5
1928—	South Side Boat Club	6:44 1-5
1929—	Penn A. C. Rowing Assn.	
1930—	Springfield Rowing Assn.	6:34 1-5
1931—	Penn A. C. Rowing Assn.	6:09
1932—	Penn A. C. Rowing Assn.	6:33 3-5
1933—	Penn A. C. Rowing Assn.	*4:10
1934—	Penn A. C. Rowing Assn.	†5:20
1935—	New York A. C.	6:59 3-5
1936—	University of Washington	¶6:05 4-5
1937—	West Side Rowing Club	6:04 2-5
1938—	West Side Rowing Club	6:39
1939—	West Side Rowing Club	6:18 1-5
1940—	Penn A. C. Rowing Assn.	6:31 2-5
1941—	Fairmount Rowing Assn.	6:54
1942—	Fairmount Rowing Assn.	6:27 3-5
1943—	Fairmount Rowing Assn.	Row Over
1944-1945—No regatta held on account of World War.		
1946—	Detroit Boat Club	7:30 2-5
1947—	West Side Rowing Club	6:04 3-5
1948—	University of California, Berkeley, Calif.	¶6:00.2
1949—	West Side Rowing Club	5:54.2
1950—	West Side Rowing Club	6:29.5
1951—	West Side Rowing Club	6:40.6
1952—	U.S. Naval Academy	5:57.7
1953—	Vesper Boat Club	6:45
(Distance changed to 2000 meters)		
1954—	Vesper Boat Club	6:55
1955—	Vesper Boat Club	6:25.4
1956—	Yale University	6:33.5
1957—	West Side A. C.	6:29.4
1958—	Vesper Boat Club	5:57.2
1959—	Lake Washington Rowing Club	5:59.2
1960—	U.S. Naval Academy	6:46.0
1961—	Lake Washington Rowing Club	5:57.4
1962—	St. Catharines Rowing Club	6:22.3
1963—	Detroit B. C.	6:05.6
1964—	Harvard University—Laconia Rowing Assn., Cambridge, Mass., Laconia, N.H.	6:23
1965—	Vesper Boat Club	6:28.4
1966—	St. Catharines Rowing Club	6:07.3
1967—	New Zealand R. A., New Zealand	5:43.7
1968—	St. Catharines R. C.	6:00.0
1969—	Union B. C. Ecorse B. C., Boston, Mass., Ecorse, Mich.	
1970—	Vesper B. C.	5:42.8
1971—	Union B. C.	5:59.4
1972—	Vesper B. C.	6:05.8
1973—	Potomac	6:24.5
1974—	N.A.A.O. National Camp	6:01.87

1975—	N.A.A.O. National Camp	5:53.08
1976—	Vesper B. C.	6:19.3
1977—	Penn A. C.	6:32.1
1978—	Penn A. C.	5:39.9
1979—	U. of Penn.	5:41.21

X-Race Rowed with one turn †Distance, 1 Mile *Distance, 1/4 Mile ¶Distance, 2000 Meters

Intercollegiate Rowing
Association Championships, 1895-1979

In 1895 Columbia, Cornell and Pennsylvania chose a four-mile straightaway on the Hudson above Poughkeepsie for what has come to be the oldest and largest regatta in the country. Frustrated by the reluctance of Harvard and Yale to accept any other entries in their race at New London, the other three colleges were seeking to acquire for their rowing the continuity and permanence which an annual fixture seemed to guarantee. The regatta got off to a shaky start: Cornell's first crew had gone to Henley with Pop Courtney; Penn's shell was so damaged by wash from a passing tug that the race had to be postponed a day; the Penn crew sank before the finish. Yet the event was a great success. The railroad ran a train of observation cars on the west bank and Columbia's victory touched off a memorable celebration. A Freshman race was added in 1896; in 1914 the JV crews first raced.

In time, three to six other crews asked to join in every year. As the numbers grew, rough water, tide and unequal lanes made the Hudson less satisfactory. Eventually (1969) the IRA found a new home on Lake Onandaga at Syracuse. The four-mile distance, despite its tradition, proved anachronistic. In 1969 the Olympic distance of 2000 meters won out, which made heats possible. The addition of races for Pairs and IVs have given the Regatta (where now over 20 colleges will enter some crews) a broader appeal and usefulness.

1895 (June 24) Hudson River, Poughkeepsie

Varsity (4 miles): 1. Columbia, 2. Cornell, 3. Pennsylvania (21 m 25.0s).

1896 (June 24, 26) Hudson River, Poughkeepsie

Varsity (4 miles): 1. Cornell, 2. Harvard, 3. Pennsylvania, 4. Columbia (19m 59.0s).

Freshman (2 miles): 1. Cornell, 2. Harvard, 3. Pennsylvania, 4. Columbia (10m 18.0s).

1897 (June 23, 25) Hudson River, Poughkeepsie

Varsity (4 miles): 1. Cornell, 2. Yale, 3. Harvard (20m 34.0s).

Freshman (2 miles): 1. Yale, 2. Harvard, 3. Cornell (9m 19.5s).

1897 (June 30, July 2) Poughkeepsie

Varsity (4 miles): 1. Cornell, 2. Columbia, 3. Pennsylvania (20m 47.8s).

Freshman (2 miles): 1. Cornell, 2. Columbia, 3. Pennsylvania (9m 21.2s).

1898 (July 2) Saratoga Lake, New York

Varsity (3 miles): 1. Pennsylvania, 2. Cornell, 3. Wisconsin, 4. Columbia (15m 51.5s).

Freshman (2 miles): 1. Cornell, 2. Columbia, 3. Pennsylvania (10m 57.6s).

1899 (June 26, 27) Hudson River,
    Poughkeepsie

Varsity (4 miles): 1. Pennsylvania, 2. Wisconsin, 3. Cornell, 4. Columbia (20m 4.0s).

Freshman (2 miles). 1. Cornell, 2. Columbia, 3. Pennsylvania (9m 55.0s).

1900 (June 30) Hudson River,
    Poughkeepsie

Varsity (4 miles): 1. Pennsylvania, 2. Wisconsin, 3. Cornell, 4. Columbia, 5. Georgetown (19m 44.6s).

Freshman (2 miles): 1. Wisconsin, 2. Pennsylvania, 3. Cornell, 4. Columbia (9m 45.4s).

1901 (July 2) Hudson River,
    Poughkeepsie

Varsity (4 miles): 1. Cornell, 2. Columbia, 3. Wisconsin, 4. Georgetown, 5. Syracuse, 6. Pennsylvania (18m 53.2s).

Freshman (2 miles): 1. Pennsylvania, 2. Cornell, 3. Columbia, 4. Syracuse (10m 20.2s).

1902 (June 21) Hudson River,
    Poughkeepsie

Varsity (4 miles): 1. Cornell, 2. Wisconsin, 3. Columbia, 4. Pennsylvania, 5. Syracuse, 6. Georgetown (19m 5.6s).

Freshman (2 miles): 1. Cornell, 2. Wisconsin, 3. Columbia, 4. Syracuse, 5. Pennsylvania (9m 39.8s).

1903 (June 26) Hudson River,
    Poughkeepsie

Varsity (4 miles): 1. Cornell, 2. Georgetown, 3. Wisconsin, 4. Pennsylvania, 5. Syracuse, 6. Columbia (18m 57.0s).

Freshman (2 miles): 1. Cornell, 2. Syracuse, 3. Wisconsin, 4. Columbia, 5. Pennsylvania (9m 18.0s).

1904 (June 28) Hudson River,
    Poughkeepsie

Varsity (4 miles): 1. Syracuse, 2. Cornell, 3. Pennsylvania, 4. Columbia, 5. Georgetown, 6. Wisconsin (20m 22.6s).

Freshman (2 miles): 1. Syracuse, 2. Cornell, 3. Pennsylvania, 4. Columbia (10m 1.0s).

1905 (June 28) Hudson River,
    Poughkeepsie

Varsity (4 miles): 1. Cornell, 2. Syracuse, 3. Georgetown, 4. Columbia, 5. Pennsylvania, 6. Wisconsin (20m 29.0s).

Freshman (2 miles): 1. Cornell, 2. Syracuse, 3. Columbia, 4. Pennsylvania (9m 39.2s).

1906 (June 23) Hudson River,
    Poughkeepsie

Varsity (4 miles): 1. Cornell, 2. Pennsylvania, 3. Syracuse, 4. Wisconsin, 5. Columbia, 6. Georgetown (19m 36.8s).

Freshman (2 miles): 1. Syracuse, 2. Cornell, 3. Wisconsin, 4. Columbia, 5. Pennsylvania (9m 51.6s).

1907 (June 26) Hudson River,
    Poughkeepsie

Varsity (4 miles): 1. Cornell, 2. Columbia, 3. Navy, 4. Pennsylvania, 5. Wisconsin, 6. Georgetown, 7. Syracuse (20m 2.4s).

Freshman (2 miles): 1. Wisconsin, 2. Syracuse, 3. Pennsylvania, 4. Columbia, 5. Cornell (9m 58.0s).

1908 (June 27) Hudson River,
    Poughkeepsie

Varsity (4 miles): 1. Syracuse, 2. Columbia, 3. Cornell, 4. Pennsylvania, 5. Wisconsin (19m 24.2s).

Freshman (2 miles): 1. Cornell, 2. Syracuse, 3. Columbia, 4. Wisconsin, 5. Pennsylvania (9m 29.6s).

1909 (July 2) Hudson River,
    Poughkeepsie

Varsity (4 miles): 1. Cornell, 2. Columbia, 3. Syracuse, 4. Wisconsin, 5. Pennsylvania (19m 2.0s).

Freshman (2 miles): 1 Cornell, 2. Syracuse, 3. Pennsylvania, 4. Wisconsin, 5. Columbia (9m 11.6s).

1910 (June 25) Hudson River,
    Poughkeepsie

Varsity (4 miles): 1. Cornell, 2. Pennsylvania, 3. Columbia, 4. Syracuse, 5. Wisconsin (20 m 42.2s).

Freshman (2 miles): 1. Cornell, 2. Columbia, 3. Syracuse, 4. Pennsylvania, 5. Wisconsin (10m 40.2s).

1911 (June 27) Hudson River, Poughkeepsie

Varsity (4 miles): 1. Cornell, 2. Columbia, 3. Pennsylvania, 4. Wisconsin, 5. Syracuse (20m 10.8s).

Freshman (2 miles): 1. Columbia, 2. Cornell, 3. Syracuse, 4. Pennsylvania, 5. Wisconsin (10m 13.2s).

1912 (June 29) Hudson River, Poughkeepsie

Varsity (4 miles): 1. Cornell, 2. Wisconsin, 3. Columbia, 4. Syracuse, 5. Pennsylvania, 6. Stanford (19m 31.4s).

Freshman (2 miles): 1. Cornell, 2. Wisconsin, 3. Syracuse, 4. Pennsylvania, 5. Columbia (9m 31.4s).

1913 (June 21) Hudson River, Poughkeepsie

Varsity (4 miles): 1. Syracuse, 2. Cornell, 3. Washington, 4. Wisconsin, 5. Columbia, 6. Pennsylvania (19m 28.6s).

Freshman (2 miles): 1. Cornell, 2. Wisconsin, 3. Syracuse, 4. Pennsylvania, 5. Columbia (10m 4.8s).

1914 (June 26) Hudson River, Poughkeepsie

Varsity (4 miles): 1. Columbia, 2. Pennsylvania, 3. Cornell, 4. Syracuse, 5. Washington, 6. Wisconsin (19m 37.8s).

Junior Varsity (2 miles): 1. Cornell, 2. Columbia, 3. Pennsylvania, 4. Syracuse (11m 15.6s).

Freshman (2 miles): 1. Cornell, 2. Syracuse, 3. Pennsylvania, 4. Wisconsin, 5. Columbia (10m 26.0s).

1915 (June 28) Hudson River, Poughkeepsie

Varsity (4 miles): 1. Cornell, 2. Stanford, 3. Syracuse, 4. Columbia, 5. Pennsylvania (19m 36.6s).

Junior Varsity (2 miles): 1. Cornell, 2. Pennsylvania, 3. Columbia (10m 0.2s).

Freshman (2 miles): 1. Syracuse, 2. Cornell, 3. Columbia, 4. Pennsylvania (9m 29.6s).

1916 (June 17, 19) Hudson River, Poughkeepsie

Varsity (4 miles): 1. Syracuse, 2. Cornell, 3. Columbia, 4. Pennsylvania (20m 15.4s).

Junior Varsity (2 miles): 1. Syracuse, 2. Cornell, 3. Columbia, 4. Pennsylvania (11m 15.4s).

Freshman (2 miles): 1. Cornell, 2. Syracuse, 3. Pennsylvania, 4. Columbia (11m 5.8s).

1920 (June 19) Lake Cayuga, New York

Varsity (2 miles): 1. Syracuse, 2. Cornell, 3. Columbia, 4. Pennsylvania (11m 2.6s).

Junior Varsity (2 miles): 1. Cornell, 2. Syracuse, 3. Pennsylvania, 4. Columbia (10m 45.6s).

Freshman (2 miles): 1. Cornell, 2. Syracuse, 3. Pennsylvania, 4. Columbia (10m 45.4s).

1921 (June 22) Hudson River, Poughkeepsie

Varsity (3 miles): 1. Navy, 2. California, 3. Cornell, 4. Pennsylvania, 5. Syracuse, 6. Columbia (14m 7.0s).

Junior Varsity (2 miles): 1. Cornell, 2. Pennsylvania, 3. Syracuse, 4. Columbia (10m 38.0s).

Freshman (2 miles): 1. Cornell, 2. Syracuse, 3. Pennsylvania, 4. Columbia (10m 32.0s).

1922 (June 26) Hudson River, Poughkeepsie

Varsity (3 miles): 1. Navy, 2. Washington, 3. Syracuse, 4. Cornell, 5. Columbia, 6. Pennsylvania (13m 33.6s).

Junior Varsity (2 miles): 1. Cornell, 2. Columbia, 3. Syracuse, 4. Pennsylvania (9m 0.8s).

Freshman (2 miles): 1. Syracuse, 2. Cornell, 3. Columbia, 4. Pennsylvania (9m 20.2s).

1923 (June 28) Hudson River, Poughkeepsie

Varsity (3 miles): 1. Washington, 2. Navy, 3. Columbia, 4. Syracuse, 5. Cornell, 6. Pennsylvania (14m 3.2s).

Junior Varsity (2 miles): 1. Syracuse, 2. Cornell, 3. Columbia, 4. Pennsylvania (9m 50.0s).

Freshman (2 miles): 1. Cornell, 2. Washington, 3. Syracuse, 4. Pennsylvania, 5. Columbia (9m 27.8s).

1924 (June 17) Hudson River, Poughkeepsie

Varsity (3 miles): 1. Washington, 2. Wisconsin, 3. Cornell, 4. Pennsylvania, 5. Syracuse, 6. Columbia (15m 2.0s).

Junior Varsity (2 miles): 1. Pennsylvania, 2. Washington, 3. Columbia, 4. Syracuse, 5. Cornell (10m 36.4s).

Freshman (2 miles): 1. Pennsylvania, 2. Cornell, 3. Syracuse, 4. Columbia (10m 22.6s).

1925 (June 22) Hudson River, Poughkeepsie

Varsity (4 miles): 1. Navy, 2. Washington, 3. Wisconsin, 4. Pennsylvania, 5. Cornell, 6. Syracuse, 7. Columbia (19m 24.8s).

Junior Varsity (2 miles): 1. Washington, 2. Cornell, 3. Pennsylvania, 4. Syracuse, 5. Columbia (10m 26.0s).

Freshman (2 miles): 1. Syracuse, 2. Pennsylvania, 3. Columbia, 4. Cornell, 5. Wisconsin (9m 59.0s).

1926 (June 28) Hudson River, Poughkeepsie

Varsity (4 miles): 1. Washington, 2. Navy, 3. Syracuse, 4. Pennsylvania, 5. Columbia, 6. California, 7. Wisconsin, 8. Cornell (19m 28.6s).

Junior Varsity (3 miles): 1. Washington, 2. Pennsylvania, 3. California, 4. Syracuse, 5. Cornell, 6. Columbia (15m 40.2s).

Freshman (2 miles): 1. Columbia, 2. Cal-

ifornia, 3. Syracuse, 4. Pennsylvania, 5. Cornell (11 28.6s).

1927 (June 29) Hudson River, Poughkeepsie

Varsity (4 miles): 1. Columbia, 2. Washington, 3. California, 4. Navy. 5. Cornell, 6. Syracuse, 7. Pennsylvania (20m 57.0s).

Junior Varsity (3 miles): 1. Washington, 2. Columbia, 3. California, 4. Pennsylvania, 5. Cornell (15m 12.8s).

Freshman (2 miles): 1. Navy, 2. Syracuse, 3. Columbia, 4. Cornell, 5. Pennsylvania, 6. California, 7. Wisconsin (9m 45.0s).

1928 (June 19) Hudson River, Poughkeepsie

Varsity (4 miles): 1. California, 2. Columbia, 3. Washington, 4. Cornell, 5. Navy, 6. Syracuse, 7. Pennsylvania (18m 35.8s).

Junior Varsity (3 miles): 1. Navy, 2. Cornell, 3. Syracuse, 4. Washington, 5. Columbia, 6. Pennsylvania (14m 18.2s).

Freshman (2 miles): 1. Navy, 2. Cornell, 3. Syracuse, 4. Washington, 5. Pennsylvania, 6. Columbia, 7. California (9m 42.0s).

1929 (June 24) Hudson River, Poughkeepsie

Varsity (4 miles): 1. Columbia, 2. Washington, 3. Pennsylvania, 4. Navy, 5. Wisconsin (unplaced—MIT, Syracuse, California, and Cornell swamped in order listed), (22m 58.0s).

Junior Varsity (3 miles): 1. Cornell, 2. Columbia, 3. Navy, 4. Washington, 5. Syracuse, 6. Pennsylvania (15m 21.2s).

Freshman (2 miles): 1. Syracuse, 2. California, 3. Cornell, 4. Navy, 5. Columbia, 6. MIT, 7. Pennsylvania (10m 23.6s).

1930 (June 26) Hudson River, Poughkeepsie

Varisty (4 miles): 1. Cornell, 2. Syracuse, 3. MIT, 4. California, 5. Columbia, 6. Washington, 7. Pennsylvania, 8. Wisconsin (unplaced—Navy swamped) (21m 42.0s).

Junior Varsity (3 miles): 1. Cornell, 2. Washington, 3. Columbia, 4. Syracuse, 5. Pennsylvania, 6. Navy (16m 39.0s).

Freshman (2 miles): 1. Syracuse, 2. Cornell, 3. Columbia, 4. Pennsylvania, 5. Washington, 6. Navy, 7. California, 8. MIT (11m 18.2s).

1931 (June 16) Hudson River, Poughkeepsie

Varsity (4 miles): 1. Navy, 2. Cornell, 3. Washington, 4. California, 5. Syracuse, 6. Pennsylvania, 7. Columbia, 8. Wisconsin, 9. MIT (18m 54.2s).

Junior Varsity (3 miles): 1. Syracuse, 2. California, 3. Cornell, 4. Columbia, 5. Navy, 6. Pennsylvania (14m 29.6s).

Freshman (2 miles): 1 Washington, 2. Cornell, 3. Syracuse, 4. Navy, 5. Columbia, 6. Pennsylvania, 7. MIT (9m 49.8s).

1932 (June 20) Hudson River, Poughkeepsie

Varsity (4 miles): 1. California, 2. Cornell, 3. Washington, 4. Navy, 5. Syracuse, 6. Columbia, 7. Pennsylvania, 8. MIT (19m 55.0s).

Junior Varsity (3 miles): 1. Syracuse, 2. California, 3. Cornell, 4. Columbia, 5. Navy, 6. Pennsylvania (14m 29.6s).

Freshman (2 miles): 1. Syracuse, 2. Navy, 3. Cornell, 4. California, 5. Pennsylvania, 6. Columbia, 7. MIT (10m 59.0s).

1934 (June 16) Hudson River, Poughkeepsie

Varsity (4 miles): 1. California, 2. Washington, 3. Navy, 4. Cornell, 5. Pennsylvania, 6. Syracuse, 7. Columbia (19m 44.0s).

Junior Varsity (3 miles): 1. Syracuse, 2. Navy, 3. Cornell, 4. California, 5. Columbia (15m 40.6s).

Freshman (2 miles): 1. Washington, 2. Syracuse, 3. Cornell, 4. Pennsylvania, 5. Columbia, 6. Rutgers (10m 50.0s).

1935 (June 18) Hudson River, Poughkeepsie

Varsity (4 miles): 1. California, 2. Cornell,

3. Washington, 4. Navy, 5. Syracuse, 6. Pennsylvania, 7. Columbia (18m 52.0s).

Junior Varsity (3 miles): 1. Washington, 2. Navy, 3. Cornell, 4. Syracuse (14m 58.8s).

Freshman (2 miles): 1. Washington, 2. California, 3. Navy, 4. Columbia, 5. Syracuse.

1936 (June 22) Hudson River, Poughkeepsie

Varsity (4 miles): 1. Washington, 2. California, 3. Navy, 4. Columbia, 5. Cornell, 6. Pennsylvania, 7. Syracuse (19m 9.6s).

Junior Varsity (3 miles): 1. Washington, 2. Navy, 3. Cornell, 4. Columbia, 5. Syracuse (14m 42.2s).

Freshman (2 miles): 1. Washington, 2. California, 3. Navy, 4. Cornell, 5. Syracuse, 6. Columbia (10m 19.6s).

1937 (June 22) Hudson River, Poughkeepsie

Varsity (4 miles): 1. Washington, 2. Navy, 3. Cornell, 4. Syracuse, 5. California, 6. Columbia, 7. Wisconsin (18m 33.6s).

Junior Varsity (3 miles): 1. Washington, 2. Navy, 3. Cornell (13m 44.0s).

Freshman (2 miles): 1. Washington, 2. California, 3. Syracuse, 4. Cornell, 5. Navy, 6. Columbia (9m 15.4s).

1938 (June 27) Hudson River, Poughkeepsie

Varsity (4 miles): 1. Navy, 2. California, 3. Washington, 4. Columbia, 5. Wisconsin, 6. Cornell, 7. Syracuse (18m 19.0s).

Junior Varsity (3 miles): 1. Washington, 2. California, 3. Navy, 4. Syracuse, 5. Cornell, 6. Columbia (13m 49.2s).

Freshman (2 miles): 1. California, 2. Washington, 3. Syracuse, 4. Columbia, 5. Cornell (9m 30.4s).

1939 (June 17) Hudson River, Poughkeepsie

Varsity (4 miles): 1. California, 2. Washington, 3. Navy, 4. Cornell, 5. Syracuse, 6. Wisconsin, 7. Columbia (18m 12.6s).

Junior Varsity (3 miles): 1. Syracuse, 2.

Washington, 3. California, 4. Navy, 5. Cornell, 6. Columbia, (13m 56.6s).

Freshman (2 miles): 1. Washington, 2. Columbia, 3. Cornell, 4. Syracuse, 5. California, 6. Wisconsin (9m 31.0s).

1940 (June 18) Hudson River, Poughkeepsie

Varsity (4 miles): 1. Washington, 2. Cornell, 3. Syracuse, 4. Navy, 5. California, 6. Columbia, 7. Wisconsin, 8. Princeton (22m 42.0s).

Junior Varsity (3 miles): 1. Washington, 2. Navy, 3. California, 4. Syracuse, 5. Columbia, 6. Cornell (No time Ta.).

Freshman (2 miles): 1. Cornell, 2. Princeton, 3. Syracuse, 4. Columbia (10m 55.4s).

1941 (June 25) Hudson River, Poughkeepsie

Varsity (4 miles): 1. Washington, 2. California, 3. Cornell, 4. Syracuse, 5. Princeton, 6. Wisconsin, 7. Rutgers, 8. MIT, 9. Columbia (22m 42.0s).

Junior Varsity (3 miles): 1. California, 2. Washington, 3. Cornell, 4. Columbia (14m 40.0s).

Freshman (2 miles): 1. Cornell, 2. Wisconsin, 3. Syracuse, 4. Princeton, 5. MIT, 6. Columbia (9m 57.7s).

1947 (June 21) Hudson River, Poughkeepsie

Varsity (3 miles): 1. Navy, 2. Cornell, 3. Washington, 4. California, 5. Princeton, 6. Pennsylvania, 7. (3 way tie) MIT, Syracuse, Wisconsin, 10. Rutgers, 11. Columbia (13m 59.2s).

Junior Varsity (3 miles): 1. California, 2. Navy, 3. Cornell, 4. Washington, 5. Syracuse, 6. Pennsylvania (14m 30.3s).

Freshman (2 miles): 1. Washington, 2. Syracuse, 3. Navy, 4. Princeton, 5. Cornell, 6. Pennsylvania, 7. Columbia (9m 40.3s).

1948 (June 22) Hudson River, Poughkeepsie

Varsity (3 miles): 1. Washington, 2. California, 3. Navy, 4. Cornell, 5. MIT, 6. Princeton, 7. Pennsylvania, 8. Wisconsin, 9. Syracuse, 10. Columbia, 11. Rutgers (14m 6.4s).

Junior Varsity (3 miles): 1. Washington, 2. California, 3. Navy, 4. Pennsylvania, 5. Columbia, 6. Cornell, 7. MIT, 8. Syracuse (14m 28.6s).

Freshman (2 miles): 1. Washington, 2. Navy, 3. Wisconsin, 4. MIT, 5. Princeton, 6. Cornell, 7. Columbia, 8. Rutgers, 9. Pennsylvania, 10. Syracuse (9m 46.9s).

1949 (June 25) Hudson River, Poughkeepsie

Varsity (3 miles): 1. California, 2. Washington, 3. Cornell, 4. Navy, 5. Princeton, 6. Pennsylvania, 7. Wisconsin, 8. Columbia, 9. Syracuse, 10. Stanford, 11. MIT, 12. Rutgers (14m 42.6s).

Junior Varsity (3 miles): 1. Washington, 2. Navy, 3. California, 4. Pennsylvania, 5. Princeton, 6. Cornell, 7. Syracuse, 8. MIT, 9. Columbia (16m).

Freshman (2 miles): 1. Washington, 2. Cornell, 3. Wisconsin, 4. Princeton, 5. Pennsylvania, 6. MIT, 7. Columbia, 8. Navy, 9. Syracuse (9m 40.2s).

1950 (June 17) Ohio River, Marietta

Distance for Varsity and Junior Varsity races shortened because of flood conditions.

Varsity (2 miles): 1. Washington, 2. California, 3. Wisconsin, 4. Stanford, 5. MIT, 6. Columbia, 7. Cornell, 8. Pennsylvania, 9. Princeton, 10. Syracuse, 11. Rutgers, 12. Navy (8m 7.5s).

Junior Varsity (2 miles): 1. Washington, 2. California, 3. Navy, 4. Princeton, 5. Cornell, 6. Syracuse, 7. Pennsylvania, 8. Columbia, 9. MIT (8m 10.4s).

Freshman (1-7/8 miles): 1. Washington, 2. Princeton, 3. Cornell, 4. Pennsylvania, 5. Wisconsin, 6. Boston U., 7. Navy, 8. Columbia, 9. Rutgers, 10. MIT, 11. Syracuse (7m 13.2s).

1951 (June 16) Ohio River, Marietta

Distance for Varsity and Junior Varsity races shortened because of flood conditions.

Varsity (2 miles): 1. Wisconsin, 2. Washington, 3. Princeton, 4. California, 5. Pennsylvania, 6. MIT, 7. Stanford, 8. Syracuse, 9. Cornell, 10. Columbia, 11. Navy, 12. Boston U. (7m 50.5s).

Junior Varsity (2 miles): 1. California, 2. Washington, 3. Columbia, 4. Cornell, 5. Marietta, 6. Pennsylvania, 7. Princeton (unplaced—Navy sank at start, after shearing off Princeton rudder. (8m 5.1s).

Freshman (2 miles): 1. Washington, 2. MIT, 3. Navy, 4. Princeton, 5. Columbia, 6. Cornell, 7. Wisconsin (unplaced—Pennsylvania failed to row after mishap) (8m 5.4s).

1952 (June 21) Onondaga Lake, Syracuse

Varsity (3 miles): 1. Navy, 2. Princeton, 3. Cornell, 4. Wisconsin, 5. California, 6. Columbia, 7. Washington, 8. Stanford, 9. Pennsylvania, 10. MIT, 11. Syracuse (15m 8.1s).

Junior Varsity (3 miles): 1. Navy, 2. Washington, 3. California, 4. Pennsylvania, 5. Cornell, 6. Princeton, 7. Columbia, 8. Syracuse (15m 37.2s).

Freshman (2 miles): 1. Navy, 2. Cornell, 3. Princeton, 4. Syracuse, 5. Pennsylvania, 6. Columbia, 7. MIT, 8. Wisconsin (10m 16.9s).

1953 (June 20) Onondaga Lake, Syracuse

Varsity (3 miles): 1. Navy, 2. Cornell, 3. Washington, 4. Wisconsin, 5. Columbia, 6. California, 7. Pennsylvania, 8. Princeton, 9. Syracuse, 10 MIT, 11. Stanford (15m 29.6s).

Junior Varsity (3 miles): 1. Washington, 2. Navy, 3. Cornell, 4. Wisconsin, 5. Columbia, 6. California, 7. Syracuse, 8. Pennsylvania, 9. Princeton (16m 30.6s).

Freshman (2 miles): 1. Washington, 2.

Cornell, 3. Princeton, 4. Navy, 5. Wisconsin, 6. Syracuse, 7. MIT, 8. Pennsylvania, 9. Columbia (10m 55.4s).

1954 (June 19) Onondaga Lake, Syracuse

Varsity (3 miles): 1. Navy (disqualified), 2. Cornell, 3. Washington, 4. Wisconsin, 5. California, 6. Columbia, 7. Pennsylvania, 8. Boston U., 9. Princeton, 10. MIT, 11. Syracuse (16m 4.4s).

Junior Varsity (3 miles): 1. Cornell, 2. Navy, 3. California, 4. Washington, 5. Syracuse, 6. Columbia, 7, Princeton, 8. Pennsylvania (16m 20.6s).

Freshman (2 miles): 1. Cornell, 2. Washington, 3. Navy, 4. Princeton, 5. Syracuse, 6. Wisconsin, 7. Pennsylvania, 8. Columbia, 9. MIT (10m 18.5s).

1955 (June 18) Onondaga Lake, Syracuse

Varsity (3 miles): 1. Cornell, 2. Pennsylvania, 3. Navy, 4. Washington, 5. Stanford, 6. California, 7. Boston U., 8. Princeton, 9. Wisconsin, 10. MIT, 11. Columbia, 12. Syracuse (15m 49.9s).

Junior Varsity (3 miles): 1. Cornell, 2. Pennsylvania, 3. Navy, 4. Washington, 5. Princeton, 6. California, 7. Syracuse, 8. Wisconsin, 9. Columbia (16m 23.2s).

Freshman (2 miles): 1. Cornell, 2. Washington, 3. MIT, 4. Navy, 5. Princeton, 6. Pennsylvania, 7. Columbia, 8. Syracuse, 9. Wisconsin (10m 33.1s).

1956 (June 16) Onondaga Lake, Syracuse

Varsity (3 miles): 1. Cornell, 2. Navy, 3. Wisconsin, 4. Washington, 5. Stanford, 6. Pennsylvania, 7. Princeton, 8. Syracuse, 9. MIT, 10. California, 11. Boston U., 12. Columbia (16m 22.4s).

Junior Varsity (3 miles): 1. Washington, 2.Cornell, 3. Princeton, 4. Pennsylvania, 5. Navy, 6. California, 7. Syracuse, 8. Columbia (17m 1.5s).

Freshman (2 miles): 1. Syracuse, 2. Navy, 3. Washington, 4. Cornell, 5. Pennsylvania,

6. Princeton, 7. Wisconsin, 8. MIT, 9. Dartmouth, 10. Columbia (11m 12.0s).

1957 (June 22) Onondaga Lake, Syracuse

Varsity (3 miles): 1. Cornell, 2. Pennsylvania, 3. Stanford, 4. Princeton, 5. Syracuse, 6. Navy, 7. Dartmouth, 8. MIT, 9. Wisconsin, 10. Columbia (15m 26.2s).

Junior Varsity (3 miles): 1. Cornell, 2. Syracuse, 3. Pennsylvania, 4. Navy, 5. Princeton, 6. Dartmouth, 7. Columbia (15m 46.8s).

Freshman (2 miles): 1. Navy, 2. MIT, 3. Cornell, 4. Rutgers, 5. Syracuse, 6. Dartmouth, 7. Boston U., 8. Princeton, 9. Pennsylvania, 10. Wisconsin, 11. Columbia (10m 25.2s).

1958 (June 21) Onondaga Lake, Syracuse

Varsity (3 miles): 1. Cornell, 2. Navy, 3. Syracuse, 4. Princeton, 5. California, 6. Pennsylvania, 7. Dartmouth, 8. Wisconsin, 9. MIT, 10. Columbia (17m 12.1s).

Junior Varsity (3 miles): 1. Cornell, 2. Syracuse, 3. California, 4. Navy, 5. Princeton, 6. Pennsylvania, 7. Dartmouth, 8. MIT, 9. Columbia (17m 33.5s).

Freshman (2 miles) 1. Cornell, 2. Navy, 3. Pennsylvania, 4. Syracuse. 5. Columbia, 6. Dartmouth, 7. Princeton, 8. MIT, 9. Wisconsin (11m 23.0s).

1959 (June 20) Onondaga Lake, Syracuse

Varsity (3 miles): 1. Wisconsin, 2. Syracuse, 3. Navy, 4. California, 5. Washington, 6. Cornell, 7. Dartmouth, 8. Pennsylvania, 9. Princeton, 10. MIT, 11. Columbia (18m 1.7s).

Junior Varsity (3 miles): 1. California, 2. Washington, 3. Pennsylvania, 4. Cornell, 5. Navy, 6. Syracuse, 7. Princeton, 8. Dartmouth, 9. Wisconsin, 10. Columbia (17m 53.5s).

Freshman (2 miles): 1. Cornell, 2. Washington, 3. Pennsylvania, 4. Syracuse, 5. Dartmouth, 6. Navy, 7. Princeton, 8. Columbia, 9. MIT, 10. Stanford (11m 47.5s).

1960 (June 18) Onondaga Lake, Syracuse

Varsity (3 miles): 1. California, 2. Navy, 3. Washington, 4. Brown, 5. Cornell, 6. Pennsylvania, 7. Dartmouth, 8. Rutgers, 9. Syracuse, 10. Princeton, 11. Wisconsin, 12. Columbia (15m 57.0s).

Junior Varsity (3 miles): 1. Cornell, 2. California, 3. Navy, 4. Washington, 5. Rutgers, 6. Pennsylvania, 7. Dartmouth, 8. Syracuse, 9. Princeton, 10. Columbia (16m 12.0s).

Freshman (2 miles): 1. Navy, 2. MIT, 3. Washington, 4. Syracuse, 5. Princeton, 6. Cornell, 7. Columbia, 8. Dartmouth, 9. Rutgers, 10. Pennsylvania (10m 45.7s).

1961 (June 17) Onondaga Lake, Syracuse

Varsity (3 miles): 1. California, 2. Cornell, 3. MIT, 4. Washington, 5. Pennsylvania, 6. Navy, 7. Brown, 8. Wisconsin, 9, Syracuse, 10. Princeton, 11. Dartmouth, 12. Rutgers, 13. Columbia (16m 49.2s).

Junior Varsity (3 miles): 1. Cornell, 2. California, 3. Navy, 4. Washington, 5. Pennsylvania, 6. MIT, 7. Princeton, 8. Columbia, 9. Dartmouth, 10. Rutgers, 11. Syracuse (17m 12.7s).

Freshman (2 miles): 1. Washington, 2. Cornell, 3. Syracuse, 4. Navy, 5. Princeton, 6. Boston U., 7. MIT, 8. Pennsylvania, 9. Wisconsin, 10. Rutgers, 11. Dartmouth, 12. Columbia (10m 51.6s).

1962 (June 16) Onondaga Lake, Syracuse

Varsity (3 miles): 1. Cornell, 2. Washington, 3. California, 4. Wisconsin, 5. Pennsylvania, 6. Dartmouth, 7. Brown, 8. Navy, 9. Columbia, 10. Princeton, 11. Syracuse, 12. MIT (17m 2.9s).

Junior Varsity (3 miles): 1. Navy, 2. Cornell, 3. Syracuse, 4. Washington, 5. Wisconsin, 6. Princeton, 7. Dartmouth, 8. Pennsylvania, 9. MIT, 10. Columbia, 11. Rutgers (16m 57.3s).

Freshman (2 miles): 1. Cornell, 2. Rutgers, 3. Washington, 4. Princeton, 5. Pennsylvania, 6. Brown, 7. Wisconsin, 8. Dartmouth, 9. Navy, 10. Syracuse, 11. Columbia, 12. MIT (11m 10.8s).

1963 (June 15) Onondaga Lake, Syracuse

Varsity (3 miles): 1. Cornell, 2. Navy, 3. MIT, 4. California, 5. Wisconsin, 6. Syracuse, 7. Washington, 8. Dartmouth, 9. Columbia, 10. Princeton, 11. Boston University, 12. Brown, 13. Marietta, 14. Pennsylvania, 15. Rutgers (17m 24.0s).

Junior Varsity (3 miles): 1. Navy, 2. Washington, 3. California, 4. Cornell, 5. MIT, 6. Wisconsin, 7. Princeton, 8. Rutgers, 9. Dartmouth, 10. Syracuse, 11. Columbia, 12. Pennsylvania (17m 28.2s).

Freshman (2 miles): 1. Navy, 2. Washington. 3. Rutgers, 4. Wisconsin, 5. Cornell, 6. Syracuse, 7. Dartmouth, 8. Princeton, 9. MIT, 10. Boston University, 11. Columbia, 12. Pennsylvania (11m 11.0s).

1964 (June 20) Onondaga Lake, Syracuse

Varsity (2000 meters): 1. California, 2. Washington, 3. Cornell, 4. Princeton, 5. MIT, 6. Navy, (2nd section), 7. Wisconsin, 8. Brown, 9. Syracuse, 10. Rutgers, 11. Dartmouth, 12. Pennsylvania (unplaced—Columbia, Georgetown) (6m 31.1s).

Junior Varsity (2000 meters): 1. Washington, 2. California, 3. Cornell, 4. MIT, 5. Navy, 6. Columbia (2nd section), 7. Wisconsin, 8. Princeton, 9. Syracuse, 10. Pennsylvania, 11. Brown, 12. Rutgers, (unplaced—Dartmouth) (6m 14.9s).

Freshman (2000 meters): 1. Wisconsin, 2. Brown, 3. Columbia, 4. Washington, 5. Cornell, 6. Syracuse, (2nd section), 7. Princeton, 8. Dartmouth, 9. Navy, 10. MIT, 11. Pennsylvania (6m 49.4s).

1965 (June 19) Onondaga Lake, Syracuse

Varsity (3 miles): 1. Navy, 2. Cornell, 3. Washington, 4. Rutgers, 5. Brown, 6. Wisconsin, 7. California, 8. Pennsylvania, 9. Stanford, 10. Dartmouth, 11. MIT, 12. Northeastern, 13. Syracuse, 14. Princeton, 15. Columbia (16m 51.3s).

Junior Varsity (3 miles): 1. Navy, 2. Wisconsin, 3. Rutgers, 4. Washington, 5. Cornell, 6. California, 7. Brown, 8. Pennsylvania, 9. Syracuse, 10. MIT, 11. Princeton, 12. Columbia (17m 7.5s).

Freshman (2 miles): 1. Navy, 2. Dartmouth, 3. Washington, 4. Cornell, 5. Pennsylvania, 6. Columbia, 7. Brown, 8. Princeton, 9. Syracuse, 10. Rutgers, 11. Wisconsin, 12. MIT (11m 3.4s).

1966 (June 18) Onondaga Lake, Syracuse

Varsity (3 miles): 1. Wisconsin, 2. Navy, 3. Princeton, 4. Brown, 5. Pennsylvania, 6. Cornell, 7. Stanford, 8. California, 9. Rutgers, 10. Syracuse, 11. Washington, 12. Dartmouth, 13. U.C.L.A., 14. MIT, and 15. Columbia (16m 3.4s).

Junior Varsity (3 miles): 1. Dartmouth, 2. Pennsylvania, 3. Cornell, 4. Washington, 5. Stanford, 6. Navy, 7. Wisconsin, 8. Rutgers, 9. Columbia, 10. Syracuse, 11. MIT, 12. Princeton, 13. Brown (16m 25.1s).

Freshman (2 miles): 1. Pennsylvania, 2. Princeton, 3. Wisconsin, 4. Navy, 5. Syracuse, 6. Columbia, 7. Dartmouth, 8. Cornell, 9. Washington, 10. Brown, 11. MIT (10m 33.5s).

1967 (June 17) Onondaga Lake, Syracuse

Varsity (3 miles): 1. Pennsylvania, 2. Wisconsin, 3. Cornell, 4. Princeton, 5. Navy, 6. Brown, 7. Washington, 8. Stanford, 9. UCLA, 10. Rutgers, 11. California, 12. Northeastern, 13. Dartmouth, 14. Syracuse, 15. MIT, 16. Columbia (16m 13.9s).

Junior Varsity (3 miles): 1. Navy, 2. Pennsylvania, 3. Wisconsin, 4. Cornell, 5. Washington, 6. Syracuse, 7. California, 8. Rutgers, 9. Stanford, 10. Princeton, 11. UCLA, 12. Brown, 13. Northeastern, 14. Dartmouth (17m 28.2s).

Freshman (2 miles): 1. Pennsylvania, 2. Rutgers, 3. Washington, 4. Princeton, 5. Wisconsin, 6. Navy, 7. Syracuse, 8. Cornell, 9. MIT, 10. Northeastern, 11. Columbia (10m 37.4s).

1968 (June 13–14–15) Onondaga Lake, Syracuse

Varsity (2000 meters): 1. Pennsylvania, 2. Washington, 3. Princeton, 4. Northeastern, 5. Rutgers, 6. Brown (6m 15.6s).

Junior Varsity (2000 meters): 1. Pennsylvania, 2. Orange Coast JC, 3. Navy, 4. Princeton, 5. Syracuse, 6. Stanford (6m 24.2s).

Freshman (2000 meters): 1. Pennsylvania, 2. Princeton, 3. Dartmouth, 4. Cornell, 5. Washington, 6. Navy (6m 18.6s).

Varsity Fours (2000 meters): 1. Cornell, 2. MIT, 3. Navy, 4. Georgetown, 5. Dartmouth, 6. Trinity (7m 24.4s).

1969 (June 12–13–14) Onondaga Lake, Syracuse

Varsity (2000 meters): 1. Pennsylvania, 2. Dartmouth, 3. Washington, 4. Wisconsin, 5. Cornell, 6. Navy (6m 30.41s).

Junior Varsity (2000 meters): 1. Cornell, 2. Wisconsin, 3. Pennsylvania, 4. UCLA, 5. Navy, 6. Northeastern (6m 26.6s).

Freshman (2000 meters): 1. dead heat between Pennsylvania and Washington, 3. Brown, 4. Syracuse, 5. Cornell, 6. Navy (6m 27.4s).

Varsity Fours (2000 meters): 1. Rutgers "A", 2. Orange Coast, 3. Cornell, 4. Wisconsin, 5. MIT "A", 6. Georgetown (7m 24.3s).

1970 (June 11–12–13) Onondaga Lake, Syracuse

Varsity (2000 meters): 1. Washington, 2. Wisconsin, 3. Dartmouth, 4. Cornell, 5. Pennsylvania, 6. Brown.

Junior Varsity (2000 meters): 1. Pennsylvania, 2. Washington, 3. Syracuse, 4. Northeastern, 5. Brown, 6. Wisconsin.

Freshman (2000 meters): 1. Brown, 2. Washington, 3. Navy, 4. Cornell, 5. Pennsylvania, 6. Rutgers, 7. Harvard.

Varsity Fours (2000 meters): 1. Rutgers, 2. MIT "A", 3. Pacific Lutheran, 4. Princeton "B", 5. Harvard, 6. Columbia.

Freshman Fours (2000 meters): 1. Cornell, 2. Navy, 3. Orange Coast, 4. MIT, 5. Columbia, 6. Dartmouth.

1971 (June 17–18–19) Onondaga Lake, Syracuse

Varsity (2000 meters): 1. Cornell, 2. Washington, 3. Pennsylvania, 4. Brown, 5. Rutgers, 6. Navy.

Junior Varsity (2000 meters): 1. Navy, 2. Northeastern, 3. Washington, 4. Wisconsin, 5. Brown, 6. Syracuse, 7. Cornell.

Freshman (2000 meters): 1. Pennsylvania, 2. Cornell, 3. Navy, 4. Syracuse, 5. Northeastern, 6. Wisconsin.

Varsity Fours (2000 meters): 1. Navy, 2. MIT, 3. California, 4. Rutgers, 5. Columbia, 6. Stanford.

Freshman Fours (2000 meters): 1. Pennsylvania, 2. Navy, 3. Wisconsin, 4. Harvard "A", 5. Princeton, 6. Boston U.

Varsity Pairs (2000 meters): 1. California, 2. Kansas State, 3. Northeastern, 4. Dartmouth, 5. MIT "A", 6. MIT "B".

1972 (June 1–2–3) Onondaga Lake, Syracuse

Varsity (2000 meters): 1. Pennsylvania, 2. Brown, 3. Wisconsin, 4. Washington, 5. Cornell, 6. Northeastern.

Junior Varisty (2000 meters): 1. Washington, 2. Wisconsin, 3. Northeastern, 4. Pennsylvania, 5. Cornell, 6. Orange Coast.

Freshman (2000 meters): 1. Wisconsin, 2. Cornell, 3. Navy, 4. California, 5. Washington, 6. Syracuse.

Varsity Fours (2000 meters): 1. UCLA, 2. Yale, 3. Oregon State, 4. Lowell Tech, 5. Pacific Lutheran, 6. Columbia.

Freshman Fours (2000 meters): 1. Princeton, 2. Santa Clara, 3. UCLA, 4. Syracuse, 5. MIT, 6. Wisconsin.

Varsity Pairs (2000 meters): 1. Trinity, 2. Morris Harvey, 3. Wisconsin, 4. Yale "A", 5. San Diego State, 6. Dartmouth "A".

1973 (May 31, June 1–2) Onondaga Lake, Syracuse

Varsity Eights (2000 meters): 1. Wisconsin, 2. Brown, 3. Northeastern, 4. Rutgers, 5. Pennsylvania, 6. MIT.

Junior Varsity (2000 meters): 1. Wisconsin, 2. Brown, 3. Pennsylvania, 4. Northeastern, 5. Cornell, 6. Coast Guard.

Freshman (2000 meters): 1. Wisconsin, 2. MIT, 3. Dartmouth, 4. Pennsylvania, 5. Northeastern, 6. Cornell.

Varsity Pairs (2000 meters): 1. Trinity, 2. Santa Clara, 3. Dartmouth, 4. Princeton, 5. Yale, 6. Columbia.

Varsity Fours (2000 meters): 1. UCLA, 2. Coast Guard, 3. Yale, 4. Western Washington, 5. Boston U., 6. Kansas State.

Freshman Fours (2000 meters): 1. Brown, 2. Navy, 3. Rutgers, 4. Cornell, 5. Santa Clara, 6. UCLA.

1974 (May 30–31, June 1) Onondaga Lake, Syracuse

Varsity Eights (2000 meters): 1. Wisconsin, 2. M.I.T., 3. Cornell, 4. Pennsylvania, 5. Rutgers, 6. Syracuse.

Junior Varsity (2000 meters): 1. Wisconsin, 2. Cornell, 3. Northeastern, 4. Pennsylvania, 5. M.I.T., 6. Brown, 7. Rutgers.

Freshman (2000 meters): 1. Cornell, 2. Wisconsin, 3. Syracuse, 4. Pennsylvania, 5. M.I.T., 6. Yale.

Varsity Pairs (with) (2000 meters): 1. Pennsylvania, 2. Cornell, 3. Syracuse, 4. Princeton, 5. Rollins, 6. Coast Guard, 7. Brown.

Varsity Pairs (without) (2000 meters): 1. Santa Clara, 2. Coast Guard, 3. Syracuse, 4. Yale, 5. Cornell, 6. Princeton.

Varsity Fours (with) (2000 meters): 1. Coast Guard, 2. Wisconsin, 3. Pennsylvania, 4. Princeton, 5. Nebraska, 6. M.I.T.

Varsity Fours (without) (2000 meters): 1. Coast Guard, 2. Pennsylvania, 3. Princeton, 4. Syracuse.

Freshman Fours (with) (2000 meters): 1. Princeton, 2. Northeastern, 3. Cornell, 4. Columbia, 5. Wisconsin, 6. Marist.

1975 (May 29–30–31) Onondaga Lake, Syracuse

Varsity Eights (2000 meters): 1. Wisconsin, 2. M.I.T., 3. Northeastern, 4. Cornell, 5. Rutgers, 6. Coast Guard.

Junior Varsity (2000 meters): 1. M.I.T.,
2. Northeastern, 3. Wisconsin, 4. Cornell, 5. Coast Guard, 6. Syracuse.

Freshman (2000 meters): 1. Pennsylvania, 2. Syracuse, 3. Wisconsin, 4. Rutgers, 5. California, 6. Princeton.

Varsity Fours (with) (2000 meters): 1. Oregon State, 2. Boston U., 3. Wisconsin, 4. Trinity, 5. Cornell, 6. Princeton.

Varsity Fours (without) (2000 meters): 1. Wisconsin, 2. Boston U., 3. Yale.

Varsity Pairs (with) (2000 meters): 1. Southern California, 2. Columbia, 3. Pennsylvania, 4. Cornell, 5. Wisconsin, 6. M.I.T.

Varsity Pairs (without) (2000 meters): 1. Penn "A", 2. Cornell, 3. Boston U., 4. Penn "B", 5. Rutgers, 6. Coast Guard.

Freshman Fours (with) (2000 meters) 1. Penn "B", 2. Northeastern, 3. Coast Guard, 4. Syracuse, 5. Penn "A", 6. Trinity.

1976 (June 3–4–5) Onondaga Lake, Syracuse

Varsity Eights (2000 meters): 1. California, 2. Princeton, 3. Wisconsin, 4. Pennsylvania, 5. M.I.T., 6. Syracuse.

Junior Varsity (2000 meters): 1. Pennsylvania, 2. Northeastern, 3. Cornell, 4. California, 5. Syracuse, 6. Wisconsin.

Freshman (2000 meters): 1. Syracuse, 2. Wisconsin, 3. Yale, 4. Pennsylvania, 5. Brown, 6. Princeton.

Varsity Fours (with) (2000 meters): 1. Navy, 2. Boston U., 3. Rutgers, 4. Yale, 5. Coast Guard, 6. Trinity.

Varsity Fours (without) (2000 meters): 1. Wisconsin, 2. Penn Blue, 3. Penn Red, 4. Yale, 5. Worcester Tech, 6. Columbia.

Varsity Pairs (with) (2000 meters): 1. Navy, 2. Pennsylvania.

Varsity Pairs (without) (2000 meters): 1. Rutgers, 2. Trinity, 3. Pennsylvania, 4. Yale, 5. M.I.T., 6. Boston U. "A".

Freshman Fours (with) (2000 meters): 1. Boston U., 2. Syracuse, 3. Brown, 4. Yale, 5. Wisconsin, 6. Cornell "A".

1977 (June 2-3-4) Onondaga Lake, Syracuse

Varsity Eights (2000 meters): 1. Cornell, 2. Pennsylvania, 3. California, 4. Yale, 5. Oregon State, 6. Wisconsin.

Junior Varsity (2000 meters): 1. Pennsylvania, 2. California, 3. Navy, 4. Yale, 5. Boston U., 6. Wisconsin.

Freshman Eights (2000 meters): 1. Syracuse, 2. Cornell, 3. Pennsylvania, 4. Yale, 5. Wisconsin, 6. Northeastern.

Varsity Fours (with) (2000 meters): 1. Princeton, 2. Santa Barbara, 3. Navy, 4. Rutgers, 5. Penn "A", 6. Coast Guard.

Varsity Fours (without) (2000 meters): 1. Penn "A", 2. Worcester Tech., 3. Coast Guard, 4. Syracuse, 5. Marist, 6. Dartmouth.

Varsity Pairs (with) (2000 meters): 1. Yale, 2. San Diego State, 3. Wisconsin, 4. Princeton, 5. Rutgers, 6. Syracuse.

Varsity Pairs (without) (2000 meters): 1. Wayne State, 2. Rutgers, 3. Kansas State, 4. Marist, 5. Penn "A", 6. Wisconsin.

Freshman Fours (with) (2000 meters): 1. Princeton, 2. Rutgers, 3. Yale, 4. Columbia "A", 5. Rhode Island, 6. Long Beach State.

1978 (June 1-2-3) Onondaga Lake, Syracuse

Varsity Eights (2000 meters): 1. Syracuse, 2. Brown, 3. Northeastern, 4. Pennsylvania, 5. Dartmouth, 6. California.

Junior Varsity (2000 meters): 1. Pennsylvania, 2. Northeastern, 3. Syracuse, 4. Brown, 5. Cornell, 6. Boston U.

Freshman Eights (2000 meters): 1. Syracuse, 2. Northeastern, 3. Cornell, 4. Pennsylvania, 5. Dartmouth, 6. Orange Coast.

Varsity Fours (with) (2000 meters): 1. Coast Guard, 2. Princeton, 3. Rutgers, 4. Syracuse, 5. Wisconsin, 6. Pennsylvania.

Varsity Fours (without) (2000 meters): 1. Oregon State, 2. Penn "A", 3. Wisconsin, 4. St. Joseph's, 5. Northeastern, 6. Worcester Tech.

Varsity Pairs (with) (2000 meters): 1. Rutgers, 2. Dartmouth, 3. Worcester Tech., 4. San Diego State, 5. Syracuse, 6. Pennsylvania.

Varsity Pairs (without) (2000 meters): 1. Rutgers, 2. California, 3. Columbia "A", 4. Syracuse, 5. Cornell, 6. Penn "B".

Freshman Fours (with) (2000 meters): 1. Princeton, 2. Columbia, 3. Worcester Tech., 4. Brown "A", 5. Penn "A", 6. Orange Coast.

1979 (May 31, June 1-2) Onondaga Lake, Syracuse

Varsity Eights (2000 meters): 1. Brown, 2. Wisconsin, 3. Syracuse, 4. Dartmouth, 5. Cornell, 6. Northeastern.

Junior Varsity (2000 meters): 1. Northeastern, 2. Wisconsin, 3. Syracuse, 4. Cornell, 5. Yale, 6. Dartmouth.

Freshman Eights (2000 meters): 1. Wisconsin, 2. Syracuse, 3. Northeastern, 4. Cornell, 5. Navy, 6. Brown.

Varsity Fours (with) (2000 meters): 1. Wash. State, 2. Syracuse, 3. Boston U., 4. Worcester Tech., 5. Coast Guard, 6. Purdue.

Varsity Fours (without) (2000 meters): 1. Penn., 2. San Diego, 3. Wisconsin, 4. Worc. Tech., 5. Coast Guard, 6. Northeastern.

Varsity Pairs (with) (2000 meters): 1. Princeton, 2. Northeastern, 3. Syracuse, 4. USC, 5. Worc. Tech., 6. Cornell.

Varsity Pairs (without) (2000 meters): 1. Conn. College, 2. Penn B., 3. Dartmouth, 4. Manhattan, 5. Trinity, 6. Boston U.

Freshman Fours (with) (2000 meters): 1. Rutgers, 2. Cornell, 3. Navy, 4. Wisconsin, 5. Northeastern, 6. Penn A.

California-Washington, 1903-1979

Though rowing began in the 1890s at Seattle and San Francisco, its development was slow and halting. Equipment was hard to come by, at least until the Pococks were lured to Seattle in 1912. Competition, so important to the quality of the rowing and the spirits of the oarsmen, was difficult to obtain and maintain. Until 1929 the crews endured a slow, rough trip by steamer from Seattle to San Francisco. In 1907 Washington and Stanford—fiercely determined to rival the haughty easterners at rowing—rowed the first four-mile race for VIIIs in the west; a year later, California and Washington raced in VIIIs for the first time before 10,000 spectators at Seattle. Although Stanford finished last in the first of many western trips to Poughkeepsie, in 1913 Conibear's Washington Huskies surprised the pundits with an impressive third. Meanwhile, California against Washington was emerging as the great natural rivalry on the Coast. After 1919, in alternate home and home regattas the two have regularly met. From 1907 through 1967 the distance was usually three miles for the Varsities and JV and two miles for the Freshmen. Since 1968 all crews have raced over 2000 meters.

CALIFORNIA-WASHINGTON

	V	*JV*	*Fr.*		*V*	*JV*	*Fr.*
1903	Wash			1921	Cal		Wash
1904	Cal			1922	Wash		Cal
1905	Cal			1923	Wash		Wash
1906	(Earthquake)			1924	Wash		Wash
1907	(crews swamped)			1925	Wash	Cal	Cal
1908	Wash			1926	Wash	Wash	Wash
1909	—			1927	Cal	Cal	Wash
1910	—			1928	Cal	Wash	Wash
1911	Wash			1929	Cal	Wash	Cal
1912	(Stanford, Wash, Cal)			1930	Wash		
				1931	Wash		
1913	Wash			1932	Cal		
1914	Wash			1933	Wash		
1915	(Stanford, Wash, Cal)			1934	Wash		
				1935	Wash		
1916	Wash			1936	Wash		
1917	Wash (Stan, Cal)			1937	Wash		
1918	WWI			1938	Wash		
1919	Wash		Cal	1939	Cal	Cal	Wash
1920	Wash		Wash	1940	Wash	Wash	Cal

	V	JV	Fr.		V	JV	Fr.
1941	Wash	Wash	Cal	1961	Cal	Cal	Wash
1942	Wash	Wash	Wash	1962	Wash	Wash	Wash
1943	Cal	—	Wash	1963	Wash	Wash	Wash
1945	WWII			1964	Cal	Wash	Wash
1946	Cal	Cal	—	1965	Cal	Cal	Cal
1947	Wash	Wash	Wash	1966	Wash	Wash	Wash
1948	Wash	Wash	Wash	1967	Wash	Cal	Wash
1949	Cal	Cal	Wash	1968	Wash	Wash	Wash
1950	Wash	Cal	Wash	1969	Wash	Wash	Wash
1951	Wash	Wash	Wash	1970	Wash	Cal	Wash
1952	Cal	Cal	Cal	1971	Wash	Wash	Wash
1953	Wash	Wash	Wash	1972	Wash	Wash	Wash
1954	Wash	Wash	Wash	1973	Wash	Wash	Wash
1955	Wash	Cal	Wash	1974	Cal	Wash	Wash
1956	Wash	Wash	Wash	1975	Wash	Wash	Wash
1957	Wash	Wash	Wash	1976	Wash	Cal	Wash
1958	Wash	Wash	Wash	1977	Wash	Wash	Wash
1959	Wash	Wash	Wash	1978	Wash	Wash	Wash
1960	Wash	Cal	Wash	1979	Cal	Cal	Wash

Eastern Association of Rowing Colleges, 150 lb. Sprint Rowing Championships, 1938-1979

Rowing for lightweight (150 lb.) oarsmen was started in 1916 at Pennsylvania by the Canadian sculler, Joe Wright. Over a half century later, many colleges as well as clubs in America and abroad have organized lightweight crews. In 1938 the Joseph Wright Trophy was put in competition for varsity lightweight crews. In 1946 the annual sprint championships were begun for Varsity, JV and Freshmen.

E.A.R.C. LIGHTWEIGHT CHAMPIONSHIPS

May 11, 1946 at Cambridge, Mass.

Varsity (1-5/16 miles): 1. Harvard, 2. Pennsylvania, 3. Cornell.

Junior Varsity (1-5/16 miles): 1. Harvard, 2. M.I.T., 3. Worcester.

Freshman (1-5/16 miles): No Race.

May 17, 1947 at Cambridge, Mass.

Varsity (2,000 meters): 1. Harvard, 2. Princeton, 3. Yale.

Junior Varsity (2,000 meters): 1. Princeton, 2. Harvard, 3. Yale.

Freshman (2,000 meters): 1. Princeton, 2. Harvard, 3. Yale.

May 15, 1948 at Princeton, N.J.

Varsity (1-5/16 miles): 1. Princeton, 2. Pennsylvania, 3. Harvard.

Junior Varsity (1-5/16 miles): 1. Yale, 2. Princeton, 3. Harvard.

Freshman (1-5/16 miles): 1. Harvard, 2. Yale, 3. Princeton.

May 14, 1949 at Princeton, N.J.

Varsity (1-5/16 miles): 1. Cornell, 2. Princeton, 3. Harvard.

Junior Varsity (1-5/16 miles): 1. Pennsylvania, 2. Harvard, 3. Princeton.

Freshman (1-5/16 miles): 1. Harvard, 2. Yale, 3. Cornell.

May 20, 1950 at Cambridge, Mass.

Varsity (1-5/16 miles): 1. Yale, 2. Cornell, 3. Pennsylvania.

Junior Varsity (1-5/16 miles): 1. Yale, 2. Princeton, 3. Harvard.

Freshman (1-5/16 miles): 1. Yale, 2. Columbia, 3. Princeton.

May 19, 1951 at Cambridge, Mass.

Varsity (1-5/16 miles): 1. Pennsylvania, 2. Yale, 3. Harvard.

Junior Varsity (1-5/16 miles): 1. Yale, 2. Harvard, 3. Princeton.

Freshman (1-5/16 miles): 1. Yale, 2. Princeton, 3. Cornell.

May 10, 1952 at Princeton, N.J.

Varsity (1-5/16 miles): 1. Pennsylvania, 2. Harvard, 3. Yale.

Junior Varsity (1-5/16 miles): 1. Harvard, 2. Yale, 3. M.I.T.

Freshman (1-5/16 miles): 1. Princeton, 2. M.I.T., 3. Yale.

May 16, 1953 at Princeton, N.J.

Varsity (1-5/16 miles): 1. Princeton, 2. Yale, 3. M.I.T.

Junior Varsity (1-5/16 miles): 1. Yale, 2. Princeton, 3. Harvard.

Freshman (1-5/16 miles): 1. Princeton, 2. Cornell, 3. Harvard.

May 15, 1954 at Princeton, N.J.

Varsity (1-5/16 miles): 1. M.I.T., 2. Princeton, 3. Pennsylvania.

Junior Varsity (1-5/16 miles): 1. Cornell, 2. Pennsylvania, 3. Harvard.

Freshman (1-5/16 miles): 1. Harvard, 2. Princeton, 3. Cornell.

May 14, 1955 at Cambridge, Mass.

Varsity (1-5/16 miles): 1. Pennsylvania, 2. M.I.T., 3. Princeton.

Junior Varsity (1-5/16 miles): 1. Cornell, 2. Princeton, 3. Harvard.

Freshman (1-5/16 miles): 1. Yale, 2. Harvard, 3. Princeton.

May 12, 1956 at Princeton, N.J.

Varsity (1-5/16 miles): 1. Princeton, 2. Cornell, 3. Harvard.

Junior Varsity (1-5/16 miles): 1. Cornell, 2. Harvard, 3. Navy.

Freshman (1-5/16 miles): 1. Princeton, 2. M.I.T., 3. Harvard.

May 18, 1957 at Annapolis, Md.

Varsity (1-5/16 miles): 1. Princeton, 2. Harvard, 3. Yale.

Junior Varsity (1-5/16 miles): 1. Navy, 2. Harvard, 3. Princeton.

Freshman (1-5/16 miles): 1. Navy, 2. Dartmouth, 3. Harvard.

May 17, 1958 at Cambridge, Mass.

Varsity (1-5/16 miles): 1. Harvard, 2. Cornell, 3. Princeton.

Junior Varsity (1-5/16 miles): 1. Harvard, 2. Princeton, 3. Navy.

Freshman (1-5/16 miles): 1. Harvard, 2. Cornell, 3. Dartmouth.

May 16, 1959 at Cambridge, Mass.

Varsity (1-5/16 miles): 1. Harvard, 2. Dartmouth, 3. Princeton.

Junior Varsity (1-5/16 miles): 1. Princeton, 2. Cornell, 3. Harvard.

Freshman (1-5/16 miles): 1. Harvard, 2. Princeton, 3. Columbia.

May 14, 1960 at Worcester, Mass.

Varsity (2,000 meters): 1. Harvard, 2. Navy, 3. Cornell.

Junior Varsity (2,000 meters): 1. Harvard, 2. Navy, 3. Cornell.

Freshman (2,000 meters): 1. Harvard, 2. Princeton, 3. M.I.T.

May 20, 1961 at Worcester, Mass.

Varsity (2,000 meters): 1. Harvard, 2. Cornell, 3. Navy.

Junior Varsity (2,000 meters): 1. Navy, 2. Princeton, 3. Cornell.

Freshman (2,000 meters): 1. M.I.T., 2. Cornell, 3. Harvard.

May 19, 1962 at Worcester, Mass.

Varsity (2,000 meters): 1. Cornell, M.I.T., Navy (Tie), 4. Harvard, 5. Princeton.

Junior Varsity (2,000 meters): 1. Harvard, 2. Cornell, 3. M.I.T.

Freshman (2,000 meters): 1. Harvard, 2. M.I.T., 3. Cornell.

May 18, 1963 at Worcester, Mass.

Varsity (2,000 meters): 1. Cornell, 2. M.I.T., 3. Harvard.

Junior Varsity (2,000 meters): 1. Cornell, 2. Harvard, 3. M.I.T.

Freshman (2,000 meters): 1. Harvard, 2. Cornell, 3. Princeton

*Jope Cup Points: Cornell 23, Harvard 19, M.I.T. 15, Columbia and Princeton 7, Navy 3, Dartmouth and Pennsylvania 2, Yale 1.

*First year of the award.

May 16, 1964 at Worcester, Mass.

Varsity (2,000 meters): 1. Cornell, 2. M.I.T., 3. Harvard.

Junior Varsity (2,000 meters): 1. Cornell, 2. Harvard, 3. M.I.T.

Freshman (2,000 meters): 1. Columbia, 2. Princeton, 3. Cornell and Pennsylvania (Tie).

Jope Cup Points: Cornell 21-1/2, Harvard 14, M.I.T. 12, Princeton 8, Columbia 7, Dartmouth 6, Yale 4, Pennsylvania 3-1/2, Navy 3.

May 15, 1965 at Worcester, Mass.

Varsity (2,000 meters): 1. Cornell, 2. Harvard, 3. M.I.T.

Junior Varsity (2,000 meters): 1. Harvard, 2. Cornell, 3. M.I.T.

Freshman (2,000 meters): 1. Harvard, 2. M.I.T., 3. Cornell.

Jope Cup Points: Harvard 23, Cornell 20, M.I.T. 15, Dartmouth and Yale 6, Columbia 5, Georgetown 2, Navy and Princeton 1.

May 14, 1966 at Worcester, Mass.

Varsity (2,000 meters): 1. Harvard, 2. Cornell, 3. Dartmouth.

Junior Varsity (2,000 meters): 1. Cornell, 2. Princeton, 3. Harvard.

Freshman (2,000 meters): 1. Harvard, 2. Pennsylvania, 3. Cornell.

Jope Cup Points: Cornell and Harvard 20, Pennsylvania and Princeton 10, M.I.T. 9, Dartmouth 6, Yale 2, Georgetown and Navy 1.

May 13, 1967 at Worcester, Mass.

Varsity (2,000 meters): 1. Cornell, 2. Pennsylvania, 3. Princeton.

Junior Varsity (2,000 meters): 1. Harvard, 2. Pennsylvania, 3. M.I.T.

Freshman (2,000 meters): 1. Pennsylvania, 2. Cornell, 3. Harvard.

Jope Cup Points: Pennsylvania 34, Cornell 33, Harvard 31, M.I.T. 22, Princeton 21, Columbia and Yale 19, Navy 15, Dartmouth 10, Rutgers 9.

May 11, 1968 at Worcester, Mass.

Varsity (2,000 meters): 1. Harvard, 2. Pennsylvania, 3. Cornell.

Junior Varsity (2,000 meters): 1. Harvard, 2. Pennsylvania, 3. Cornell.

Freshman (2,000 meters): 1. Harvard, 2. Pennsylvania, 3. M.I.T.

Jope Cup Points: Harvard, 38; Pennsylvania, 33; Cornell, 27; Princeton, 21;

Yale, 20; M.I.T., 17; Rutgers, 16; Navy, 13; Columbia, 11; Georgetown, 11; Dartmouth, 9.

May 10, 1969 at Worcester, Mass.

Varsity (2,000 meters): 1. Harvard 6:21.8 2. M.I.T. 6:27.7, 3. Rutgers 6:27.

Junior Varsity (2,000 meters): 1. Harvard 6:30.8, 2. Princeton 6:33.5, 3. Navy 6:36.4.

Freshman (2,000 meters): 1. Harvard 6:31.5, 2. M.I.T. 6:34.4, 3. Pennsylvania 6:37.0

Jope Cup Points: Harvard, 38; M.I.T., 27; Pennsylvania, 26; Yale, 25; Princeton, 22; Rutgers, 19; Cornell, 18; Navy, 14; Dartmouth, 7.

May 9, 1970 at Worcester, Mass.

Varsity (2,000 meters): 1. Harvard 6:06.7 2. Yale 6:15.7, 3. Princeton 6:16.3.

Junior Varsity (2,000 meters): 1. Harvard 6:24.1, 2. Yale 6:30.6, 3. Navy 6:31.1.

Freshman (2,000 meters): 1. Princeton 6:28.8, 2. Harvard 6:31.0, 3. Navy 6:32.6

Jope Cup Points: Harvard 37, Yale 30, Navy 27, M.I.T., Pennsylvania and Princeton 22 each, Cornell 17, Dartmouth 7, Rutgers 6, Columbia 4.

May 8, 1971 at Worcester, Mass.

Varsity (2,000 meters): 1. Harvard 6:39.2, 2. Columbia 6:53.2, 3. Princeton 6:55.5.

Junior Varsity (2,000 meters): 1. Harvard 7:01.5, 2. Navy 7:05.0, 3. M.I.T. 7:07.4.

Freshman (2,000 meters): 1. Harvard 7:12.2, 2. Pennsylvania 7:15.6, 3. M.I.T. 7:17.4

Jope Cup Points: Harvard 38, Princeton 27, Navy 26, Pennsylvania 25, M.I.T. 23, Columbia 19, Cornell 15, Yale 15, Rutgers 10, Dartmouth 9, Georgetown 9.

May 13, 1972 at Worcester, Mass.

Varsity (2,000 meters): 1. Harvard 6:29.5, 2. Princeton 6:38.7, 3. Navy 6:41.0.

Junior Varsity (2,000 meters): 1. Harvard 6:29.0, 2. Princeton 6:33.9, 3. Navy 6:35.8.

Freshman (2,000 meters): 1. Princeton 6:18.1, 2. Pennsylvania 6:20.6, 3. Harvard 6:24.1.

Jope Cup Points: Harvard 36, Princeton 34, Navy 25, Pennsylvania 22, Cornell 19, Yale 18, M.I.T. 18, Columbia 18, Dartmouth 15, Rutgers 10, Georgetown 3.

May 12, 1973 at Worcester, Mass.

Varsity (2,000 meters): 1. Princeton 6:15.5, 2. Harvard 6:19.5, 3. Pennsylvania 6:24.3.

Junior Varsity (2,000 meters): 1. Harvard 7:18.2, 2. Princeton 7:26.2, 3. Pennsylvania 7:26.9.

Freshman (2,000 meters): 1. Harvard 7:17.2, 2. Pennsylvania 7:25.2, 3. Princeton 7:29.

Jope Cup Points: Harvard 36, Princeton 34, Pennsylvania 30, Navy 24, Rutgers 19, Cornell 18, M.I.T. 17, Yale 15, Dartmouth 10, Columbia 5.

May 11, 1974 at Worcester, Mass.

Varsity (2,000 meters): 1. Harvard 6:28.2, 2. Pennsylvania 6:31.9, 3. M.I.T. 6:34.3.

Junior Varsity (2,000 meters): 1. Harvard 6:30.8, 2. Princeton 6:36.2, 3. Navy 6:37.8.

Freshman (2,000 meters): 1. Harvard 6:26.8, 2. Rutgers 6:31.4, 3. Dartmouth 6:31.6.

Jope Cup Points: Harvard 38, Rutgers 26, M.I.T. 25, Princeton 24, Pennsylvania 3, Navy 21, Cornell 20, Dartmouth 15, Yale 13, Columbia 2.

May 11, 1975 at Princeton, N.J.

Varsity (2,000 meters): 1. Harvard 6:00.8, 2. Navy 6:01.3, 3. Dartmouth 6:03.2.

Junior Varsity (2,000 meters): 1. Harvard 6:04.4, 2. Rutgers 6:04.7, 3. Navy 6:09.9.

Freshman (2,000 meters): 1. Harvard 6:10.7, 2. Pennsylvania 6:16.2, 3. Princeton 6:19.0.

Jope Cup Points: Harvard 38, Navy 30, Penn 28, Rutgers 25, Princeton 20, M.I.T.

18, Yale 17, Cornell 15, Dartmouth 14, Columbia 6.

May 16, 1976 at Princeton, N.J.

Varsity (2,000 meters): 1. Penn 6:25.5, 2. Harvard 6:27.5, 3. Dartmouth 6:29.6.

Junior Varsity (2,000 meters): 1. Harvard 6:39.1, 2. Navy 6:42.8, 3. Princeton 6:45.5.

Freshman (2,000 meters): 1. Yale 6:43.3, 2. Princeton 6:48.6, 3. Cornell 6:51.0

Jope Cup Points: Harvard 33, Princeton 28, Pennsylvania 27, Yale 26, Navy 22, Cornell 20, Dartmouth 18, Rutgers 14, M.I.T. 13, Columbia 6, Coast Guard 5.

May 15, 1977 at Princeton, N.J.

Varsity (2,000 meters): 1. Harvard 6:19.5, 2. Navy 6:23.7, 3. Penn 6:25.0.

Junior Varsity (2,000 meters): 1. Harvard 6:49.3, 2. Penn 6:51.8, 3. Princeton 6:52.9.

Freshman (2,000 meters): 1. Yale 6:46.7, 2. Harvard 6:49.8, 3. Cornell 6:53.8.

Jope Cup Points: Harvard 37, Princeton 27, Yale 27, Pennsylvania 24, Cornell 23, Navy 21, Rutgers 18, Dartmouth 15, M.I.T. 14, Columbia 6, Trinity 4.

May 14, 1978 at Worcester, Mass.

Varsity (2,000 meters): 1. Harvard 6:16.5, 2. Princeton 6:17.8, 3. Rutgers 6:20.1.

Junior Varsity (2,000 meters): 1. Harvard 6:08.4, 2. Penn 6:16.5, 3. Cornell 6:16.8.

Freshman (2,000 meters): 1. Dartmouth 6:26.0, 2. Navy 6:27.5, 3. Cornell 6:33.6.

Jope Cup Points: Harvard 34, Cornell 28, Princeton 26, Penn 23, Rutgers 22, Dartmouth 21, Navy 20, M.I.T. 17, Yale 17.

May 13, 1979 at Worcester, Mass.

Varsity (2,000 meters): 1. Yale 6:28.5, 2. Princeton 6:31.6, 3. Harvard 6:35.3.

Junior Varsity (2,000 meters): 1. Harvard 6:48.1, 2. Navy 6:52.5, 3. Cornell 6:55.4.

Freshman (2,000 meters): 1. Harvard

6:48.6, 2. Yale 6:49.6, 3. Princeton 6:53.2.

Jope Cup Points: Harvard 34, Yale 29, Princeton 27, Cornell 26, Navy 24, M.I.T. 21, Penn 19, Dartmouth 18, Columbia 7, Rutgers 6.

The Dad Vail Regatta, 1939-1970

Harry Emerson (Dad) Vail, one of the last of the professional scullers, coached at Wisconsin for many years where he did much to keep rowing alive in the Middle West. Conceived both to honor the memory of an old friend and to provide more competition among the newer rowing colleges, Rusty Callow presented the Dad Vail trophy in 1934. Five years later the cup became the centerpiece for a regatta. Initially for heavy VIIIs, in the 1970s IVs, pairs, light weights and women's events had been added. By 1979 there were 45 races on the first day, finals in 15 events and over 1600 rowers stirring up the Schuylkill.

DAD VAIL REGATTA

Year	Place	Distance	Varsity	JV	Freshman
May 20, 1939	Red Bank NJ	1-1/2 miles	Rutgers BU Marietta	Manhattan Rutgers Dartmouth	Rutgers Dartmouth Marietta
May 18, 1940	Springfield MA	Henley	Rutgers Marietta Springfield	Rutgers Dartmouth —	Rutgers Manhattan Dartmouth
May 17, 1941	Marietta Ohio	Henley	Rutgers Marietta BU	American International Col. Rutgers Marietta	Rutgers Marietta —
May 9, 1942	Boston	Henley	Rutgers BU American International	— — —	Rutgers Dartmouth American International
May 24, 1947	Boston	Henley	BU Dartmouth Marietta	Rutgers BU —	— — —
May 22, 1948	Boston	Henley	BU Rollins Dartmouth	BU Rutgers Dartmouth	BU Dartmouth Iona
May 21, 1949	Poughkeepsie	Henley	BU Rollins Washington and Lee	BU Rutgers Dartmouth	BU Rutgers Dartmouth

Year	Place	Distance	Varsity	JV	Freshman
May 20, 1950	Poughkeepsie	Henley	BU Rollins Dartmouth	Dartmouth BU Florida Southern	BU Dartmouth La Salle
May 19, 1951	Boston	Henley	La Salle Washington and Lee Florida Southern	Dartmouth La Salle American International	American International Dartmouth La Salle
May 10, 1952	Boston	Henley	La Salle Rollins Dartmouth	Dartmouth Amherst Brown	— — —
May 8-9, 1953	Philadelphia	Henley	La Salle Rollins Dartmouth	Dartmouth Amherst La Salle	Dartmouth — —
May 14-15, 1954	Philadelphia	Henley	Dartmouth Rollins Amherst	Dartmouth Amherst La Salle	— — —
May 13-14, 1955	Philadelphia	Henley	Dartmouth Rollins Amherst	Dartmouth Amherst —	Dartmouth Brown La Salle
May 11-12, 1956	Philadelphia	Henley	La Salle Rollins Amherst	Rollins La Salle Brown	Purdue La Salle —
May 3-4, 1957	Philadelphia	Henley	La Salle Tampa Rollins	Rollins Brown Purdue	La Salle Brown Fordham
May 9-10, 1958	Philadelphia	Henley	La Salle Fordham Tampa	Purdue La Salle Tampa	La Salle Brown Drexel Tech.
May 8-9, 1959	Philadelphia	Henley	Brown Menlo Park St. Joseph's	La Salle Tampa Rollins	St. Joseph's La Salle Fordham
May 13-14, 1960	Philadelphia	Henley	Brown St. Joseph's Purdue	St. Josephs Rollins Brown	Brown St. Joseph's La Salle
May 12-13, 1961	Philadelphia	Henley	Brown Amherst Georgetown	Brown Georgetown Marietta	Brown Fordham La Salle
May 11-12, 1962	Philadelphia	Henley	Georgetown Marietta Trinity	Georgetown Amherst Drexel	La Salle Georgetown St. Joseph's
May 12-13, 1963	Philadelphia	Henley	Marietta Georgetown Amherst	Georgetown Amherst Marietta	Fordham Georgetown Marietta

Year	Place	Distance	Varsity	JV	Freshman
May 8–9, 1964	Philadelphia	Henley	Georgetown St. Joseph's Marietta	Rollins Marietta Georgetown	Marietta Georgetown Drexel
May 7–8, 1965	Philadelphia	Henley	Northeastern Marietta Rollins	Northeastern Rollins Marietta	Northeastern Marietta St. Joseph's
May 13–14, 1966	Philadelphia	Henley	Marietta St. Joseph's Amherst	Marietta Georgetown Trinity	Marietta Fordham St. Joseph's
May 12–13, 1967	Philadelphia	Henley	Marietta Georgetown Purdue	Georgetown La Salle Trinity	Marietta La Salle Marist
May 10–11, 1968	Philadelphia	Henley	Georgetown	—	Marietta
May 9–10, 1969	Philadelphia	Henley	Georgetown St. Joseph's Trinity	Marietta Trinity Georgetown	Marietta Georgetown Trinity
May 8–9, 1970	Philadelphia	Henley	St. Joseph's Georgetown Trinity	Georgetown Marietta La Salle	Trinity Marist Georgetown
May 7–8, 1971	Philadelphia	Henley	Georgetown St. Joseph's Virginia	Marietta Massachusetts Marist	Marietta Virginia Florida Institute
May 12–13, 1972	Philadelphia	Henley	Coast Guard Rollins Marietta	Marietta Coast Guard Massachusetts	Marist Massachusetts Coast Guard
May 11–12, 1973	Philadelphia	Henley	Massachusetts Temple Coast Guard	Marietta Coast Guard Massachusetts	Marietta Massachusetts Drexel
1974	Philadelphia	Henley	Massachusetts		
May 9–10, 1975	Philadelphia	Henley	Coast Guard Massachusetts Ithaca	Coast Guard Massachusetts St. Joseph's	Florida Inst. Tech. Trinity Marietta
May 7–8, 1976	Philadelphia	Henley	Coast Guard Trinity Rollins	Marietta Coast Guard Florida Inst. Tech.	Marietta Coast Guard Trinity
May 14–15, 1977	Philadelphia	Henley	—	—	Ithaca
May 12–13, 1978	Philadelphia	Henley	Coast Guard Florida Inst. Tech. Drexel	Coast Guard Florida Inst. Tech. Trinity	Marietta Ithaca Merchant Marine

Year	Place	Distance	Varsity	JV	Freshman
May 11–12, 1979	Philadelphia	Henley	Coast Guard Marietta Florida Inst. Tech.	Massachusetts Coast Guard Western Ontario	Florida Inst. Tech. Marietta

Eastern Association of Rowing Colleges, Heavyweight Sprint Rowing Championships, 1946-1979

The name reveals the earlier attitude of American colleges to any race much shorter than two miles, but over the last 25 years the 2000 meter distance has won American as well as international acceptance. The distance allows both heats and finals to be held in one day. Since the Sprints returned to Worcester, both heavyweight and 150s can race over the same course the same day which yields as many as 27 races. With the exception of Wisconsin (who in 1946 did not have as much regional competition as is available today) the entries are confined to eastern crews. Sixteen colleges are now racing in the Sprints.

E.A.R.C. HEAVYWEIGHT CHAMPIONSHIPS

May 11, 1946, at Annapolis

Varsity (1-3/4 miles): 1. Wisconsin 9:12.8, 2. Navy, 3. Columbia.

Junior Varsity (1-3/4 miles): 1. Princeton 10:37, 2. Cornell, 3. M.I.T.

Freshman (1-3/4 miles): No Race.

Rowe Cup Points: Wisconsin 10, Princeton 8, Navy 6, Cornell 5, Columbia 3, M.I.T. 2.

May 17, 1947, at Princeton

Varsity (2,000 meters): 1. Harvard 6:05, 2. Navy, 3. Cornell.

Junior Varsity (2,000 meters): 1. Harvard 6:14, 2. Pennsylvania, 3. Princeton.

Freshman (2,000 meters): 1. Princeton 6:18.2, 2. Navy, 3. Yale.

Rowe Cup Points: Harvard 18, Navy 10, Princeton 8, Pennsylvania 5, Cornell 3, Yale 1.

May 15, 1948, at Cambridge

Varsity (2,000 meters): 1. Harvard 6:15.4, 2. Yale, 3. Navy.

Junior Varsity (2,000 meters): 1. Yale 6:21.6, 2. Pennsylvania, 3. M.I.T.

Freshman (2,000 meters): 1. Yale 6:20.2, 2. Navy, 3. M.I.T.

Rowe Cup Points: Yale 20, Harvard 10, Navy 7, Pennsylvania 5, M.I.T. 3.

May 14, 1949, at Syracuse

Varsity (2,000 meters): 1. Harvard 6:48.4, 2. Pennsylvania, 3. Princeton.

Junior Varsity (2,000 meters): 1. Harvard 6:50.9, 2. Princeton, 3. Yale.

Freshman (2,000 meters): 1. Harvard 6:52.5, 2. M.I.T., 3. Princeton.

Rowe Cup Points: Harvard 24, Princeton 9, Pennsylvania 6, M.I.T. 4, Yale 2.

May 13, 1950, at Annapolis

Varsity (2,000 meters): 1. M.I.T. 6:28.8, 2. Harvard, 3. Princeton.

Junior Varsity (2,000 meters): 1. Princeton 6:33, 2. Harvard, 3. Navy.

Freshman (2,000 meters): 1. Harvard 6:47.1, 2. Princeton, 3. Boston U.

Rowe Cup Points: Harvard 17, Princeton 15, M.I.T. 10, Navy 2, Boston U. 1.

May 19, 1951, at Princeton

Varsity (2,000 meters): 1. Yale 6:18.4, 2. Harvard, 3. Princeton.

Junior Varsity (2,000 meters): 1. Harvard 6:28, 2. Cornell, 3. Princeton.

Freshman (2,000 meters): 1. Navy 6:24.4, 2. Princeton, 3. Cornell.

Rowe Cup Points: Harvard 14, Yale 10, Princeton 9, Cornell 6, Navy 6.

May 17, 1952, at Princeton

Varsity (2,000 meters): 1. Navy 6:03.7, 2. Wisconsin, 3. Harvard.

Junior Varsity (2,000 meters): 1. Navy 6:11.8, 2. Pennsylvania, 3. Harvard.

Freshman (2,000 meters): 1. Navy 6:15.7, 2. Harvard, 3. Cornell.

Rowe Cup Points: Navy 24, Harvard 9, Wisconsin 6, Pennsylvania 5, Cornell 1.

May 16, 1953, at Washington, D.C.

Varsity (2,000 meters): 1. Navy 6:07.4, 2. Harvard, 3. Wisconsin.

Junior Varsity (2,000 meters): 1. Navy 6:15.7, 2. Cornell, 3. Harvard.

Freshman (2,000 meters): 1. Cornell 6:20.5, 2. Harvard, 3. Princeton.

Rowe Cup Points: Navy 18, Harvard 12, Cornell 11, Wisconsin 3, Princeton 1.

May 15, 1954, at Washington, D.C.

Varsity (2,000 meters): 1. Navy 6:03.4*, 2. Yale, 3. Pennsylvania.

Junior Varsity (2,000 meters): 1. Navy 6:21.4, 2. Harvard, 3. Princeton.

Freshman (2,000 meters): 1. Cornell 6:15.8, 2. Yale, 3. Boston U.

Rowe Cup Points: Navy 18*, Yale 10, Cornell 6, Harvard 5, Pennsylvania 4, Princeton 2, Boston U. 1.

*The Navy varsity crew disqualified because of ineligible coxswain. No trophies awarded.

May 14, 1955, at Washington, D.C.

Varsity (2,000 meters): 1. Pennsylvania 6:00.6, 2. Cornell, 3. Columbia.

Junior Varsity (2,000 meters): 1. Cornell 6:06.1, 2. Yale, 3. Harvard.

Freshman (2,000 meters): 1. Harvard 6:08.7, 2. Cornell, 3. Princeton.

Rowe Cup Points: Cornell 18, Pennsylvania 10, Harvard 8, Yale 5, Columbia 3, Princeton 1.

May 12, 1956, at Washington, D.C.

Varsity (2,000 meters): 1. Cornell 6:10.0, 2. Yale, 3. Pennsylvania.

Junior Varsity (2,000 meters): 1. Cornell 6:15.9, 2. Pennsylvania, 3. Navy.

Freshman (2,000 meters): 1. Navy 6:35.6, 2. Yale, 3. Princeton.

Rowe Cup Points: Cornell 18, Yale 10, Navy 8, Pennsylvania 8, Princeton 1.

May 18, 1957, at Princeton

Varsity (2,000 meters): 1. Cornell 6:11.8, 2. Yale 6:11.9, 3. Navy 6:23.8.

Junior Varsity (2,000 meters): 1. Cornell 6:20.4, 2. Navy 6:23.4, 3. Syracuse 6:27.0.

Freshman (2,000 meters): 1. Yale 6:30.1, 2. Harvard 6:33.3, 3. Cornell 6:33.6.

Rowe Cup Points: Cornell 19, Yale 12, Navy 8, Harvard 4, Syracuse 2.

May 17, 1958, at Princeton

Varsity (2,000 meters): 1. Yale 5:54.4, 2. Penn 5:59.8, 3. Harvard 6:01.1.

Junior Varsity (2,000 meters): 1. Penn 6:04.4, 2. Navy 6:04.5, 3. Cornell 6:10.1.

Freshman (2,000 meters): 1. Harvard 5:57.4, 2. Penn 5:58.3, 3. Navy 5:59.4.

Rowe Cup Points: Pennsylvania 21, Harvard 15, Yale 15, Navy 12, Cornell 10, Syracuse 5, Columbia 1.

May 16, 1959, at Princeton

Varsity (2,000 meters): 1. Harvard 6:03.1, 2. Syracuse 6:03.7, 3. Yale 6:07.9.

Junior Varsity (2,000 meters): 1. Penn 6:12.2, 2. Navy 6:15.1, 3. Cornell 6:15.3.

Freshman (2,000 meters): 1. Cornell

6:13.8, 2. Harvard 6:20.6, 3. Pennsylvania 6:28.6.

Rowe Cup Points: Harvard 18, Pennsylvania 16, Cornell 14, Navy 11, Syracuse 8, Yale 7, Princeton 4, Dartmouth 1.

May 14, 1960, at Worcester Mass.

Varsity (2,000 meters): 1. Cornell 6:33.5, 2. Harvard 6:38.4, 3. Navy 6:38.9.

Junior Varsity (2,000 meters): 1. Cornell 6:37.5, 2. Navy 6:43.0, 3. Harvard 6:43.8.

Freshman (2,000 meters): 1. Navy 6:44.1, 2. Cornell 6:45.1, 3. Harvard 6:48.5.

Rowe Cup Points: Cornell 23, Navy 19, Harvard 16, Syracuse 7, Pennsylvania 4, Yale 3, M.I.T. 2, Dartmouth 1.

May 20, 1961, at Worcester, Mass.

Varsity (2,000 meters): 1. Navy 6:01.5, 2. Cornell 6:01.9, 3. M.I.T. 6:08.9.

Junior Varsity (2,000 meters): 1. Navy 6:01.9, 2. Cornell 6:02.5, 3. Harvard 6:07.3.

Freshman (2,000 meters): 1. Syracuse 6:05.8, 2. Navy 6:06.3, 3. Cornell 6:06.7.

Rowe Cup Points: Navy 23, Cornell 18, M.I.T. and Syracuse 11, Harvard and Princeton 5, Brown and Yale 3.

May 19, 1962, at Worcester Mass.

Varsity (2,000 meters): 1. Penn & Yale (tie) 6:09.3, 2. Cornell 6:12.9, 3. Harvard 6:13.5.

Junior Varsity (2,000 meters): 1. Cornell 6:16.4, 2. Yale 6:19.4, 3. Syracuse 6:22.4.

Freshman (2,000 meters): 1. Cornell 6:11.8, 2. Harvard 6:15.8, 3. Yale 6:17.2.

Rowe Cup Points: Cornell 21, Yale 19, Harvard 11, Penn 9, Syracuse 6, M.I.T. 4, Rutgers and Wisconsin 3.

May 18, 1963, at Worcester, Mass.

Varsity (2,000 meters): 1. Ratzeburg 6:21.3 (GUEST CREW), 2. Cornell 6:25.3, 3. Yale 6:31.3, 4. Princeton 6:35.0.

Junior Varsity (2,000 meters): 1. Cornell

6:30.4, 2. Navy 6:31.6, 3. Yale 6:33.4.

Freshman (2,000 meters): 1. Harvard 6:25.6, 2. Cornell 6:29.6, 3. Navy 6:33.1.

Rowe Cup Points: Cornell 23, Yale 12, Navy 10, Harvard 9, Princeton 8, Wisconsin 4, Brown, Dartmouth, and M.I.T. 3, Columbia and Syracuse 2.

May 16, 1964, at Worcester, Mass.

Varsity (2,000 meters): 1. Harvard 6:32.0, 2. Cornell 6:36.0, 3. Yale 6:37.5.

Junior Varsity (2,000 meters): 1. Harvard 6:35.1, 2. Yale 6:40.8, 3. M.I.T. 6:42.1.

Freshman (2,000 meters): 1. Cornell 6:41.5, 2. Harvard 6:44.4, 3. Boston Univ. 6:44.9.

Rowe Cup Points: Harvard 23, Cornell 17, Yale 14, M.I.T. 7, Boston 4, Wisconsin 4, Brown, Navy, and Syracuse 3, Princeton 1.

May 15, 1965, at Worcester, Mass.

Varsity (2,000 meters): 1. Harvard 6:10.4, 2. Cornell 6:20.1, 3. Brown 6:23.4.

Junior Varsity (2,000 meters): 1. Harvard 6:19.4, 2. Navy 6:22.2, 3. Cornell 6:22.8.

Freshman (2,000 meters): 1. Harvard 6:22.9, 2. Cornell 6:24.1, 3. Navy 6:31.5.

Rowe Cup Points: Harvard 25, Cornell 17, Navy 13, Brown 6, Yale 5, M.I.T. 5, Pennsylvania 3, Wisconsin 2, Boston Univ. 2, Rutgers 1.

May 14, 1966, at Worcester, Mass.

Varsity (2,000 meters): 1. Harvard 6:20.8, 2. Brown 6:24.2, 3. Cornell 6:25.0.

Junior Varsity (2,000 meters): 1. Harvard 6:33.2, 2. Yale 6:37.3, 3. Wisconsin 6:39.8.

Freshman (2,000 meters): 1. Pennsylvania 6:31.2, 2. Harvard 6:36.3, 3. Boston Univ. 6:41.9.

Rowe Cup Points: Harvard 23, Yale 13, Pennsylvania 10, Brown 8, Cornell 7, Boston Univ. and Wisconsin 4, Princeton and Rutgers 3, M.I.T. and Northeastern 2.

May 13, 1967, at Worcester, Mass.

Varsity (2,000 meters): 1. Harvard 6:06.2, 2. Pennsylvania 6:13.8, 3. Northeastern 6:14.6.

Junior Varsity (2,000 meters): 1. Pennsylvania 6:20.4, 2. Yale 6:25.6, 3. Harvard 6:27.4.

Freshman (2,000 meters): 1. Harvard 6:13.1, 2. Rutgers 6:18.3, 3. Princeton 6:18.7.

Rowe Cup Points: Harvard 38, Pennsylvania 34, Yale 27, Northeastern 22, Princeton 20, Cornell, Navy and Syracuse 19, B.U. 14, Brown and Rutgers 13, M.I.T. 9, Wisconsin 6, Columbia 2, Dartmouth 1.

May 11, 1968, at Worcester, Mass.

Varsity (2,000 meters): 1. Harvard 5:54.5, 2. Pennsylvania 5:57.9, 3. Yale 6:05.3.

Junior Varsity (2,000 meters): 1. Pennsylvania 6:03.5, 2. Harvard 6:06.9, 2. Yale 6:14.1.

Freshman (2,000 meters): 1. Pennsylvania 6:06.8, 2. Harvard 6:11.2, 3. Princeton 6:16.6.

Rowe Cup Points: Pennsylvania 39, Harvard 38, Northeastern 29, Yale 28, Princeton 24, Rutgers 22, Navy 16, Wisconsin 15, Cornell 15, Dartmouth 10, Brown 7, Syracuse 7, M.I.T. 5, Boston U., 1.

May 10, 1969, at Worcester, Mass.

Varsity (2,000 meters): 1. Harvard 6:01.3, 2. Pennsylvania 6:06.1, 3. Princeton 6:07.9.

Junior Varsity (2,000 meters): 1. Harvard 6:17.0, 2. Cornell 6:21.1, 3. Navy 6:22.6.

Freshman (2,000 meters): 1. Pennsylvania 6:15.0, 2. Harvard 6:16.7, 3. Syracuse 6:37.2.

Rowe Cup Points: Harvard 40, Pennsylvania 35, Cornell 26, Princeton 18, Syracuse 18, Yale 18, Wisconsin 17, Navy 17, Northeastern 16, Rutgers 14, Brown 12, Columbia 12, Dartmouth 9, M.I.T. 4.

May 9, 1970, at Worcester, Mass.

Varsity (2,000 meters): 1. Harvard 5:54.1, 2. Pennsylvania 5:55.9, 3. Princeton 5:59.0.

Junior Varsity (2,000 meters): 1. Pennsylvania 6:07.0, 2. Harvard 6:07.2, 3. Wisconsin 6:07.3.

Freshman (2,000 meters): 1. Navy 6:13.5, 2. Harvard 6:17.0, 3. Brown, 6:18.6.

Rowe Cup Points: Harvard 38, Pennsylvania 36, Brown 28, Navy 24, Wisconsin 22, Cornell 20, Syracuse 18, Princeton 15, Dartmouth and Northeastern 11, Columbia 10, Rutgers 9, Yale 7, M.I.T. 2, Boston University 1.

May 8, 1971, at Worcester, Mass.

Varsity (2,000 meters): 1. Navy 6:17.2, 2. Rutgers 6:20.2, 3. Harvard 6:20.8.

Junior Varsity (2,000 meters): 1. Brown 6:23.2, 2. Navy 6:26.2, 3. Harvard 6:28.4.

Freshman (2,000 meters): 1. Navy 6:34.1, 2. Harvard 6:39.6, 3. Syracuse 6:41.6.

Rowe Cup Points: Navy 39, Harvard 33, Brown 27, Northeastern 25, Pennsylvania 23, Wisconsin 23, Cornell 17, Rutgers 15, Syracuse 15, Dartmouth 14, Boston U. 12, Princeton 8, Yale 5.

May 13, 1972, at Worcester, Mass.

Varsity (2,000 meters): 1. Northeastern 6:11.5, 2. Brown 6:15.8, 3. Harvard 6:16.1.

Junior Varsity (2,000 meters): 1. Harvard 6:32.0, 2. Navy 6:35.9, 3. Wisconsin 6:36.7.

Freshman (2,000 meters): 1. Harvard 6:26.0, 2. Navy 6:33.1, 3. Northeastern 6:33.8.

Rowe Cup Points: Harvard 37, Northeastern 33, Navy 28, Brown 28, Cornell 28, Wisconsin 27, Pennsylvania 23, M.I.T. 11, Rutgers 9, Boston U. 9, Syracuse 8, Princeton 7, Yale 6, Dartmouth 2.

May 12, 1973, at Worcester, Mass.

Varsity (2,000 meters): 1. Northeastern 5:54.6, 2. Wisconsin 5:57, 3. Harvard 5:57.9.

Junior Varsity (2,000 meters): 1. Harvard 6:12.6, 2. Wisconsin 6:13.2, 3. Northeastern 6:18.2.

Freshman (2,000 meters): 1. Dartmouth 7:22.1, 2. M.I.T. 7:27.6, 3. Harvard 7:28.4.

Rowe Cup Points: Harvard 35, Northeastern 34, Wisconsin 28, Brown 25, Cornell 25, Pennsylvania 23, M.I.T. 22, Dartmouth 14, Navy 11, Syracuse 11, Rutgers 10, Yale 10, Boston U. 7.

May 11, 1974, at Worcester, Mass.

Varsity (2,000 meters): 1. Harvard 6:02.8, 2. Wisconsin 6:07.6, 3. Northeastern 6:10.8.

Junior Varsity (2,000 meters): 1. Harvard 6:09.5, 2. Wisconsin 6:11.2, 3. Cornell 6:21.7.

Freshman (2,000 meters): 1. Cornell 6:11.4, 2. Harvard 6:12.2, 3. Rutgers 6:17.8.

Rowe Cup Points: Harvard 40, Wisconsin 34, Cornell 29, M.I.T. 24, Northeastern 22, Pennsylvania 20, Syracuse 19, Navy 17, Rutgers 16, Princeton 10, Boston U. 8, Brown 7, Yale 6, Dartmouth 4.

May 11, 1975, at Princeton, N.J.

Varsity (2,000 meters): 1. Harvard 5:43.6, 2. M.I.T. 5:47.0, 3. Wisconsin 5:51.5.

Junior Varsity (2,000 meters): 1. Harvard 5:54.4, 2. Cornell 5:57.0, 3. Navy 6:03.6.

Freshman (2,000 meters): 1. Pennsylvania 5:54.7, 2. Princeton 6:01.0, 3. Harvard 6:02.2.

Rowe Cup Points: Harvard 39, Northeastern 28, Cornell 28, M.I.T. 23, Pennsylvania 23, Wisconsin 22, Rutgers 20, Syracuse 17, Princeton 16, Navy 13, Yale 11, Boston U. 9, Brown 4, Dartmouth 3.

May 16, 1976, at Princeton, N.J.

Varsity (2,000 meters): 1. Harvard 6:07.4, 2. Wisconsin 6:11.1, 3. Penn 6:12.9.

Junior Varsity (2,000 meters): 1. Penn 6:23.1, 2. Navy 6:26.1, 3. Northeastern 6:27.3.

Freshman (2,000 meters): 1. Harvard 6:20.7, 2. Yale 6:25.7, 3. Princeton 6:28.9.

Rowe Cup Points: Harvard 36, Pennsylvania 33, Wisconsin 32, Princeton 26, Navy 26, Yale 22, Boston University 20, Northeastern 15, Brown 14, Syracuse 11, Coast Guard 11, Dartmouth 6, Cornell 2, Rutgers 2, Columbia 1, MIT 1.

May 15, 1977, at Princeton, N.J.

Varsity (2,000 meters): 1. Harvard 6:03.7, 2. Penn 6:06.0, 3. Cornell 6:09.8.

Junior Varsity (2,000 meters): 1. Penn 6:18.7, 2. Yale 6:23.3, 3. Harvard 6:27.8.

Freshman (2,000 meters): 1. Penn 6:19.5, 2. Princeton 6:19.9, 3. Yale 6:20.0.

Rowe Cup Points: Penn 39, Harvard 34, Yale 31, Syracuse 28, Cornell 21, Brown 19, Wisconsin 18, Navy 15, Northeastern 15, Princeton 15, Dartmouth 9, M.I.T. 7, Rutgers 5.

May 14, 1978, at Worcester, Mass.

Varsity (2,000 meters): 1. Yale 5:58.0, 2. Harvard 6:00.9, 3. Syracuse 6:05.9.

Junior Varsity (2,000 meters): 1. Harvard 6:03.1, 2. Yale 6:07.9, 3. Northeastern 6:09.5.

Freshman (2,000 meters): 1. Northeastern 6:02.5, 2. Harvard 6:04.4, 3. Syracuse 6:05.9.

Rowe Cup Points: Harvard 38, Yale 35, Northeastern 31, Syracuse 28, Penn 25, Navy 18, Rutgers 13, Brown 12, Princeton 12, B.U. 10, Cornell 10, Wisconsin 9, Columbia 7, Dartmouth 6, MIT 2.

May 13, 1979, at Worcester, Mass.

Varsity (2,000 meters): 1. Yale 6:09.1, 2. Harvard 6:12.5, 3. Dartmouth 6:13.2.

Junior Varsity (2,000 meters): 1. Yale 6:25.4, 2. Northeastern 6:28.8, 3. Harvard 6:29.3.

Freshman (2,000 meters): 1. Yale 6:34.3, 2. Northeastern 6:35.8, 3. Wisconsin 6:37.

Rowe Cup Points: Yale 41, Harvard 32, Northeastern 26, Wisconsin 24, Syracuse 22, Dartmouth 21, Cornell 18, Brown 17, Navy 14, Rutgers 10, Penn 10, MIT 9, Boston Univ. 7, Princeton 3, Columbia 2.

Western Sprints, 1961-1979

Over the last twenty years two factors have combined to increase the number of college races or regattas each spring. First, the spread of trailers and rigs has greatly simplified the transfer of racing shells; and second, the readiness of oarsmen and coaches to substitute the shorter 2000 meter Olympic distance for the traditionally longer distances (a mile and three quarters, two miles or even longer). Racing over the sprint distance has made possible two races a day and a complete regatta with heats, repechages and finals over a weekend. The Western Sprints began in 1961. The increased competition which they provided helped to spread rowing up and down the West coast. By the early 70s the Sprints had entries from a dozen or more colleges, in 14 events for women, light weights as well as heavies. By 1977 the Sprints had become unworkable: 800 men and women, from 30 colleges, trying to race in 63 events over two days! The lack of a permanent site (such as the Eastern Sprints were eventually to find at Worcester) continued to produce unpredictable, often unsatisfactory conditions. The pressure was relieved in 1978 by the withdrawal of the larger colleges from the Sprints to race in the Pac-8 Championships. Together the two regattas provided the Western crews with the same range of opportunities as the Dad Vail and the Eastern Sprints.

WESTERN SPRINTS

	Varsity		*JV*		*Freshman*	
May 20, 1961	Washington	6:32.3	California	6:39.7	Washington	6:44.2
Seattle	California	6:32.5	Washington	6:43.7	Oregon State	7:12.2
2000 meters	Brit. Columbia	6:37.9	Brit. Columbia	6:48.9	UCLA	7:55.6
May 19, 1962	Washington	6:41.8	Washington	6:16.0		
Long Beach	Brit. Columbia	6:45.1	Brit. Columbia	6:21.2		
2000 meters	California	6:19.6	California	6:22.3		
May 18, 1963	Washington	6:40	Washington	6:44	California	7:10
Stanford	California	6:41.5	California	6:54.0	Stanford	7:14
2000 meters	Long Beach St.	6:52	Long Beach St.	6:54.5	Long Beach St.	7:17
May 23, 1964	California	6:11.7	Washington	6:25.6	Long Beach St.	6:24.6
San Diego	Washington	6:12.0	California	6:27.5		
2000 meters	Long Beach St.	6:15.5	Brit. Columbia	6:44.2		
May 22, 1965	Washington	6:34.2	Washington	6:26.0	Washington	6:52
Seattle	Brit. Columbia	6:35.1	California	6:32	Long Beach St.	7:01.2
2000 meters	California	6:37.3	Oregon State	6:43.0	Orange State	7:17.8
May 21, 1966	Washington	6:51	Washington	5:59.6	Oregon State	8:24

Valleja, Cal.	Stanford	6:54.3	Orange State	6:03.9	California	8:26
2000 meters	California	6:55.6	Brit. Columbia	6:06.4	Stanford	
May 20, 1967	UCLA	6:15.2	Stanford	6:27.3	Stanford	6:30.9
Long Beach	Washington	6:19.8	California	6:27.3	UC-Irvine	6:37.1
2000 meters	Stanford	6:22.5	Orange Coast	6:28.3	UCLA	6:37.2
May 18, 1968	Washington	5:56.7	Orange Coast	6:07.2	Washington	6:10.8
Seattle	UCLA	6:00.4	Washington	6:11.9	Stanford	6:11.7
2000 meters	California	6:09.1	California	6:12.5	Oregon State	6:25.2
May 17, 1969	Washington	6:18.7	UCLA	6:27.5	Washington	6:40.0
San Diego	Stanford	6:23.5	Washington	6:28.5	Stanford	6:45.3
2000 meters	UC Irvine	6:26.9	UC Irvine	6:36.9	California	6:46.2
May 16, 1970	UCLA	5:59.4	Washington	6:22.4	Washington	6:16.5
Long Beach	Washington	6:03.3	Orange State	6:22.4	UCLA	6:22.6
2000 meters	Long Beach St.	6:08.5	UCLA		Orange Coast	6:27
May 23, 1971	Washington	6:06.3	Washington	6:14.4	Washington	6:10.3
Seattle	Brit. Columbia	6:12.3	UCLA	6:22.4	UCLA	6:17.3
2000 meters	Loyola	6:13.1	Orange Coast	6:22.45	Orange Coast	6:19.7
May 20, 1972	Washington	5:58.5	Orange County	6:09	Washington	6:17
Long Beach	Long Beach St.	6:00	Washington	6:14	California	6:23
2000 meters	Brit. Columbia	6:05	Oregon State	6:19	Santa Clara	6:26
May 19, 1973	Washington	5:51.4	Washington	5:58	Washington	6:05
Los Gatos	California	5:57.5	California	6:07.4	USC	6:11.8
2000 meters	Oregon State	5:59.0	UC Irvine	6:10.1	California	6:12.8
May 18, 1974	Washington	6:01.39	Washington	6:15.17	Washington	6:10.4
Burnaby, B. C.	U.C. Irvine	6:03.87	California	6:25.25	California	6:19.8
2000 meters	California	6:06.64	Orange Coast	6:28.4	Stanford	6:24.0
May 14, 1975	Washington	6:00.7	Washington	6:13.6	California	6:12.1
Long Beach	Oregon State	6:11.1	Orange Coast	6:15.8	Washington	6:12.2
2000 meters	California	6:14.3	California	6:20.8	UCLA	6:20
May 14, 1976	Washington	6:03.2	California	6:02.1	Washington	6:09.2
San Marino	California	6:07.5	Orange Coast	6:04	California	6:11.9
2000 meters	Oregon State	6:08.5	Washington	6:06.5	Orange Coast	6:16.7
May 14, 1977	Brit. Columbia	6:02.8	Orange Coast	6:11.1	Orange Coast	6:14.9
Newport Beach,	Santa Barbara	6:00.7	Brit. Columbia	6:18.7	UC San Diego	6:19
Western Sprints,	UC Irvine	6:10.2	Stanford	6:21.3	Stanford	6:31.5
2000 meters						
May 22, 1977	Washington	6:34.4	California	6:39.5	Washington	6:37.3
Redwood Shores	Oregon State		Washington		California	
Pac-8, 2000						
meters						
May 20, 1978	Brit. Columbia	6:01.2	California		Orange Coast	6:58.4
Los Gatos	California		Irvine	6:34	California	
Western Sprints	Irvine	6:06.8	Orange Coast	6:37.1	Irvine	6:59.1
2000 meters	Long Beach	6:14.3	Birt. Columbia	6:44.5	California-San	
					Diego	7:23.9

		Varsity		*JV*		*Freshman*	
May 20, 1978	Washington	5:57.8	Washington	6:12.8	Washington	6:15.9
Seattle	California	5:58.1	California	6:17.1	UCLA	6:22.6
Pac-8, 2000	Oregon State	6:06.2	UCLA	6:19.4	California	6:26.7
meters						
May 19, 1979	California	5:53.6	Washington	6:08.3	Washington	6:23.4
Redwood	Washington	5:56.5	California	6:10.1	California	6:27.5
Shores, Pac-10	Oregon State	6:14.9	UCLA	6:31.8	Oregon State	6:37.2
2000 meters						
May 19, 1979	California-Irvine		Occidental		Occidental	
Los Gatos	California-San Diego		California-San Diego		California-Irvine	
Western Sprints	Stanford		California-Irvine		Stanford	

National Women's Rowing Association, Annual Championships, 1966-1979

The phenomenal growth of women's rowing in America is reflected in the movement and expansion of NWRA's Championships. Oakland, Princeton, Seattle, and Detroit represent some of the sites; the participants come from more than seventy clubs and schools; four days are needed to run off over twenty events. The racing over 1000 meters includes events for schools and clubs, singles, doubles, quads, IVs with and VIIIs, for crews of various size and experience. The NWRA also holds regional championships each year. Here are the results of some of the events in the Nationals.

LIGHTWEIGHT FOUR WITH COXSWAIN

1966—	Green Lake Junior C. A. Seattle, Wash.	5:00.0
1967—	Green Lake Junior C. A.	4:41.0
1968—	Lake Merritt R. C. Oakland, Ca.	4:15.2
1969—	Lake Merritt R. C.	4:21.1
1970—	Univ. of Wash. Seattle, Wash.	4:19.8
1971—	Univ. of Wash.	4:10.5
1972—	Lake Merritt R. C.	4:23.3
1973—	U. of Washington	3:37.4
1974—	Boston Univ. Boston, MA	4:27.2
1975—	UCLA	3:47.6
1976—	College B. C., Philadelphia, PA	3:56.0
1977—	College B. C.	3:59.2
1978—	Lake Washington R. C.	3:45.2
1979—	Pioneer Valley R. A.	3:40.2

HEAVYWEIGHT (OPEN) FOUR WITH COXSWAIN

1966—	Lake Merritt R. C.	4:32.0
1967—	Philadelphia Girls R. C., Philadelphia, Pa.	4:15.1
1968—	Lake Washington R. C., Seattle, Wash.	4:10.6
1969—	Lake Washington R. C.	4:13.3
1970—	Lake Washington R. C.	4:16.2
1971—	Vesper B. C., Philadelphia, Pa.	4:12.1
1972—	College B. C.	4:07.1
1973—	Vesper B. C.	3:27.9
1974—	Boston University	4:05.9
1975—	Vesper B. C.	3:30.6
1976—	College B. C.	3:42.4

1977—	Vesper B. C.	3:35.2
1978—	Vesper B. C.	3:32.3
1979—	Vesper B. C.	3:26.2

LIGHTWEIGHT QUAD WITH COXSWAIN

1966—	Lake Merritt R. C.	4:55.0
1967—	Lake Merritt R. C.	4:20.6
1968—	Lake Merritt R. C.	4:23.0
1969—	Philadelphia Girls, R. C.	4:19.8
1970—	Lake Merritt R. C.	4:13.4
1971—	Blood Street Sculls, Old Lyme, Conn.	4:31
1972—	University of Wash.	4:25.8
1973—	LBRA, RBC, UBC, LWRC/Baldwin	4:23.8
1974—	LBRA, LWRC/RBC/LBSU	5:10.1
1975—	Vesper B. C.	3:52.5
1976—	L.B.R.A.	3:46.4
1977—	LWRC, LBRA	3:48.1
1978—	Lake Washington R. C.	3:45.2
1979—	DART/SDRT, CAMB/LWRC	3:42

HEAVYWEIGHT (OPEN) QUAD WITH COXSWAIN

1966—	Lake Washington R. C.	4:16.7
1967—	Philadelphia Girls R. C.	4:16.4
1968—	Philadelphia Girls R. C.	4:04.5
1969—	Philadelphia Girls R. C.	4:09.0
1970—	Lake Merritt R. C.	4:21.3
1971—	Vesper B. C.	4:26.4
1972—	Long Beach R. A., Long Beach, Calif.	3:51.4
1973—	Vesper B. C.	3:53.6
1974—	L.B.R.A.	4:00.0
1975—	Equipe de Quebec, Canada	3:36.4
1976—	USA Team	3:31.2
1977—	L.B.R.A.	3:36.2
1978—	U. Mass/Yale/Mission Bay/Dart.	3:35.2
1979—	Yale	3:06.2

LIGHTWEIGHT SINGLE

1966—	Lake Washington R. C. (S. Garret)	5:37.7
1967—	Lake Merritt R. C.	4:51.2
1968—	Lake Washington R. C. (S. Garret)	4:20.3
1969—	Lake Merritt R. C.	4:43.4
1970—	Vesper B. C. (K. Constant)	4:49.4
1971—	Vesper B. C. (K. Constant)	5:04.1

1972—	Vesper B. C. (K. Constant)	4:33.7
1973—	Lake Washington R. C. (S. Garret)	5:04.4
1974—	Vesper B. C. (K. Constant)	4:33
1975—	Vesper B. C. (K. Constant)	4:14.3
1976—	Mexico (Trapaga)	4:10.5
1977—	Lake Washington R. C. (J. Lennox)	4:23.0
1978—	Lake Washington R. C. (Lennox)	4:08.3
1979—	Florida Tech. (Brown)	4:01.6

HEAVYWEIGHT (OPEN) SINGLE

1966—	Lake Washington R. C. (N. Sands)	4:56.5
1967—	Philadelphia Girls R. C. (J. Becker)	5:11.4
1968—	Devon Sculls (J. Becker)	5:14.8
1969—	Lake Washington R. C. (N. Sands)	4:52.5
1970—	Vesper B. C. (K. Constant)	4:33.4
1971—	Vesper B. C. (K. Constant)	4:25.6
1972—	Long Beach R. A. (Simpson)	4:30.0
1973—	Long Beach R. A. (J. Lind)	4:11.7
1974—	Long Beach R. A. (J. Lind)	4:13.2
1975—	Equipe de Quebec	3:59.0
1976—	L.B.R.A. (J. Lind)	3:52.2
1977—	Long Beach R. A. (J. Lind)	3:57.2
1978—	Long Beach R. A. (Hansen)	3:48.1
1979—	Dartmouth R. C. (Geer)	3:44.2

LIGHTWEIGHT DOUBLE

1966—	Lake Merritt R. C.	5:05.4
1967—	Lake Washington R. C.	4:48.3
1968—	Lake Washington R. C.	4:57.6
1969—	Lake Washington R. C.	4:37.4
1970—	Lake Merritt R. C.	4:30.8
1971—	Lake Merritt R. C.	4:46
1972—	Lake Washington/Univ. Barge	4:41.0
1973—	Philadelphia Girls R. C.	3:58.5
1974—	Vesper B. C. (E. St. Clair, S. Bromley)	4:32.4
1975—	Lake Washington R. C. (S. Bromley, J. Williams)	3:44.2
1976—	L.W.R.C. (S. Bromley, J. Lennox)	3:56.2
1977—	Lake Washington R. C. (S. Bromley, J. Lennox)	3:45.0
1978—	Lake Washington R. C.	3:42.9
1979—	Potomac B. C.	3:41.3

HEAVYWEIGHT (OPEN) DOUBLE

| 1966— | Lake Washington R. C. | 4:54.0 |
| 1967— | Philadelphia Girls R. C. (N. Farrel, E. Bayer) | 4:25.8 |

1968—	Philadelphia Girls R. C. (N. Farrel, E. Bayer)	4:46.3
1969—	Philadelphia Girls R. C. (N. Farrel, E. Bayer)	4:09.8
1970—	Vesper B. C. (J. Becker, K. Constant)	4:16.2
1971—	Vesper B. C. (J. Becker, K. Constant)	4:18.6
1972—	Long Beach R. A. (J. Lind, McCloskey)	4:03.6
1973—	Long Beach R. A. (J. Lind, McCloskey)	3:24.3
1974—	Long Beach R. A. (J. Lind, L. Hansen)	3:56.5
1975—	Equipe de Quebec (J. Lepage, E. Bourbeao)	3:44.2
1976—	L.B.R.A. (J. Lind, L. Hansen)	3:36.7
1977—	Long Beach R. A. (J. Lind, L. Hansen)	3:34.2
1978—	Long Beach R. A.	3:32.8
1979—	Dartmouth/U. Mass	3:26.4

LIGHTWEIGHT PAIR WITHOUT COXSWAIN

1968—	Lake Merritt R. C.	4:27.8
1969—	Minneapolis R. C., Minneapolis, Minn.	5:07.5
1970—	Lake Merritt R. C.	4:54.3
1971—	Lake Merritt R. C.	5:05.2
1972—	Vesper B. C. (A. Jonik, M. Jonik)	4:42.9
1973—	BDSS	4:29.0
1974—	Greenlake	4:51.6
1975—	Boston University (M. Heddy, J. Friedman)	4:07.2
1976—	College B. C.	4:09
1977—	College B. C. (S. Hochgraft, C. Fuerst)	4:08
1978—	Minnesota	4:09.2
1979—	Vesper B. C.	3:50.9

LIGHTWEIGHT EIGHT

1966—	Green Lake Junior C. A.	4:29.2
1967—	Green Lake Junior C. A.	4:15.1
1968—	Lake Merritt R. C.	3:44.0
1969—	Lake Merritt R. C.	3:55.2
1970—	Lake Merritt R. C.	3:59.3
1971—	Univ. of Wash.	4:02.4
1972—	Univ. of Wash.	3:54.1
1973—	Univ. of Washington	3:50.0
1974—	Minn.	3:58.2
1975—	B. U., U. of New Hampshire	3:27.4
1976—	Boston University	3:42.3
1977—	MBRA, ZLAC	3:29.2
1978—	College Boat Club	3:25.4
1979—	College Boat Club	3:23.1

HEAVYWEIGHT (OPEN) PAIR WITHOUT COXSWAIN

| 1966— | Lake Washington R. C. | 4:45.6 |
| 1967— | Lake Washington R. C. | 4:42.8 |

1968—	Philadelphia Girls R. C. (P. Gibson, N. Farrel)	4:04.6
1969—	Lake Washington R. C.	4:25.5
1970—	Vesper B. C. (S. Pierce, V. Helenski)	4:35.2
1971—	Vesper B. C. (S. Pierce, V. Helenski)	4:38.2
1972—	College B. C. (V. Helenski, S. Pierce)	4:25.0
1973—	College B. C.	4:16.0
1974—	Princeton Univ. (Brown, Youngholm)	4:25.6
1975—	Vesper B. C. (A. Jonik, M. Jonik)	3:55.2
1976—	L.B.R.A. (L. Hansen, C. Schneider)	3:53.5
1977—	Yale/Vesper B. C. (A. DeFrantz, A. Warner)	3:54.7
1978—	Vesper	3:47.8
1979—	Eastern Develop Camp	3:49.9

HEAVYWEIGHT (OPEN) EIGHT

1966—	Philadelphia Girls R. C.	4:07.5
1967—	Philadelphia Girls R. C.	3:44.8
1968—	Philadelphia Girls R. C.	4:07.0
1969—	Lake Washington R. C.	3:51.5
1970—	Lake Merritt	3:59.8
1971—	Vesper B. C.	3:43.4
1972—	College B. C., Philadelphia Girls R. C.	3:48.1
1973—	Radcliffe College	3:15.4
1974—	Vesper B. C.	3:42.1
1975—	Wisconsin University	3:07.3
1976—	College B. C.	3:23.4
1977—	Vesper	3:15.8
1978—	Barnaby Lake A. C.	3:07.6
1979—	Barnaby B. C.	3:01.4

HIGH SCHOOL EIGHT

1969—	Lake Merritt R. C.	4:05.0
1970—	Holy Name H. S. Oakland, Calif.	3:58.8
1971—	Baldwin School, Philadelphia, PA	4:06.2
1972—		
1973—	Baldwin School	3:44.9
1974—	Baldwin School	4:11.8
1975—	Z.L.A.C.	3:35.2
1976—	St. Paul	3:27.9
1977—	Z.L.A.C.	3:36.0
1978—	Philadelphia Girls R. C.	3:26.8
1979—	St. Catharine's Composite	3:10

American Rowing and the Henley Royal Regatta

Founded in 1839 to attract visitors to the town, the **Henley Royal Regatta** has become one of the influential, festive features of the rowing world. At one time or another almost thirty countries have sent crews to Henley, and "the delightfully illogical" length of the lovely straightaway from Temple Island almost to Henley Bridge (about a mile and 550 yards) has been copied the world over. The Regatta runs for four days in late June during which time the winners for a dozen events row through a series of eliminations to final victory. Always limited to amateurs, Henley now includes four races for VIIIs, three for IVs without, two for IVs with, one for Pairs without, one for Doubles, and one for single scullers. Over almost a century and a half the requirements for many of the trophies have inevitably changed. By 1874 the three races for IVs had dropped the cox. Only in 1963 did a race for IV with reappear, and only in 1967 was the **Ladies** opened to VIIIs from colleges overseas as well as from England.

The entry of an American sculler in 1872 began to make of Henley the international regatta it has increasingly become. The increase is seen in the contrast between the number of Americans rowing during Henley's first century as compared with the last forty years. Two Olympics (1908, 1948) have been held at Henley. Since 1946 the **Grand,** which remains one of the elite races of the world, has gone outside England 18 times in 34 races, to 7 Russian, 5 German and 5 American crews. By 1978 there were 233 entries for Henley, of which 51 were from overseas.

Event	Date of Founding	1839–1939 American Entries/Winners		1945–1979 American Entries/Winners		
GRAND VIIIs	1839	13	2	37	5	Harvard 1914, 1939, 1950, 1959 Penn 1955; Cornell 1957 Washington 1977.
LADIES' VIIIs	1845	—	—	30	3	Harvard 1973; Trinity 1977
THAMES VIIIs	1868	21	6	85	20	Browne and Nicholas 1929 Kent School 1933, 1938, 1947, 1950 Tabor Academy 1936, 1937, 1939 Princeton 1948, 1949, 1956, 1967, 1973 Penn 1951, 1952; Cornell 1967 MIT 1954, 1955; Eliot House 1964 Harvard 1958, 1959, 1960, 1966, 1971, 1972, 1976
Princess Elizabeth VIIIs Schools	1946	—	—	47	6	Tabor Academy 1965 J.E.B. Stuart H.S. 1968 Washington-Lee H.S. 1969 Kent School 1972 Holy Spirit H.S. 1974, 1976
Stewards IV without	1841	—	—	4	1	Potomac B. C. 1975
Visitors IV without	1847	1	1	14	1	Cornell 1878 Washington 1977
Wyfolds IV without	1847	2	0	24	2	Harvard 1971 Porcellian Club 1974
Prince Philip IV with	1963	—	—	22	1	Northeastern 1973
Goblets pair without	1850	—	—	29	1	Borchelt and Adams 1973
Doubles double sculls	1946	—	—	10	0	
Diamonds single sculls	1844	33	4	34	4	E. H. Ten Eyck 1897 W. M. Hoover 1922 J. W. Burk, 1938, 1939 J. B. Kelly 1947, 1949
Totals		70	13	336	44	S. Cromwell 1964; D. M. Spero 1965

American Rowing and the European and World Championships, 1893-1979: Men

By the late 19th century competitive rowing had spread from England to the continent, generating an increasing number of regattas. The first European Championships were held in Brussels in 1890. The absence of any international agreement on rules was producing such heated arguments that in 1892 representatives of five national federations (Belgium, France, Italy and Switzerland) formed the FISA or Fédération international des sociétès d'aviron, the oldest governing body for sport in the world. Their first concern was to agree upon a uniform code for boat racing and to organize international championships. As a federation of such national associations as the NAAO, FISA defines an amateur as one who is so recognized by his own association. Separated by geography as well as slow and expensive transportation, the American federation (NAAO) only joined in 1929 in order to host the 1932 Olympics. Since then American rowers have participated with increasing regularity in the European and World Championships which, together with the rowing Olympics, are under FISA's direction.

Before 1965 American oarsmen participated only occasionally in the European championships:

1930: An VIII from Penn A. C. (3 times U.S. and once Canadian champion) won the gold at the European championships at Liege; their time (5:18.2) has long been considered the fastest recorded for 2000 meters.

1949: John B. Kelly, Jr. (Vesper) won the gold at Amsterdam in the Singles.

1955: John B. Kelly, Jr. (Vesper) was fourth at Ghent.

1958: A Vesper VIII won the silver at Posnan in Poland.

1964: At Amsterdam a Vesper Pair was fourth; a Vesper Pair was seventh; a Vesper IV without was seventh. (These crews were later combined to make the Vesper 1964 VIII who took the gold at the Tokyo Olympics.) A sculler from the NYCA won the bronze.

After 1965 an American team was entered every year in the European or Worlds. Together with the Olympics this has provided an elite level regatta every year. The first six places each year are given for the races from 1965 on.

EUROPEAN CHAMPIONS: 1893–1965

	Four With	Pair	Single	Pair With	Four Without	Double	Eight
1893	Switzerland		Belgium				France
1894	France		France	Belgium			France
1895	France		Belgium	France			France
1896	France		Switzerland	Belgium			France
1897	Belgium		Belgium	Belgium			Belgium
1898	Belgium		Belgium	France		France	Belgium
1899	Belgium		France	France		Belgium	Belgium
1900	Belgium		France	France		France	Belgium
1901	Italy		France	France		France	Belgium
1902	France		Italy	Belgium		Belgium	Belgium
1903	Belgium		France	Belgium		Belgium	Belgium
1904	Belgium		Switzerland	France		France	Belgium
1905	Belgium		Als.-Lorraine	Belgium		Belgium	France
1906	Belgium		France	Italy		Belgium	Belgium
1907	Belgium		France	Belgium		Italy	Belgium
1908	Italy		France	Belgium		Belgium	Belgium
1909	Italy		Italy	Italy		Belgium	France
1910	Italy		France	Belgium		France	Belgium
1911	Switzerland		Italy	Italy		Italy	Italy
1912	Switzerland		Belgium	Switzerland		Italy	Switzerland
1913	Switzerland		Germany	France		France	Germany
1920	Switzerland		Switzerland	France		France	Switzerland
1921	Switzerland		Holland	Belgium		Holland	Switzerland
1922	France		Switzerland	Switzerland		Switzerland	France
1923	Switzerland		Switzerland	Switzerland		Switzerland	Italy
1924	Holland	Switzerland	Switzerland	Holland		Switzerland	Holland
1925	Italy	Switzerland	Holland	Switzerland	Switzerland	France	Switzerland
1926	Italy	Switzerland	Switzerland	Switzerland	Switzerland	Switzerland	Holland
1927	Italy	Italy	Italy	Italy	Italy	Switzerland	Italy
1929	Italy	Italy	Holland	Italy	Italy	Switzerland	Italy
1930	Denmark	Poland	Hungary	Italy	Italy	Switzerland	United States of America
1931	Italy	Holland	Switzerland	France	Switzerland	Switzerland	France
1932	Italy	Switzerland	Italy	Holland	Hungary	Hungary	Yugoslavia
1933	Italy	Hungary	Poland	Hungary	Denmark	France	Hungary
1934	Italy	Austria	Germany	Hungary	Germany	Switzerland	Hungary
1935	Germany	Hungary	Poland	Italy	Switzerland	Poland	Hungary
1937	Germany	Italy	Switzerland	Germany	Germany	Germany	Italy
1938	Germany	Germany	Germany	Italy	Switzerland	Italy	Germany
1947	France	Denmark	France	Hungary	Italy	Holland	Italy
1949	Italy	Sweden	U.S.A.	Italy	Italy	Denmark	Italy
1950	Denmark	Switzerland	Denmark	Italy	Italy	Denmark	Italy
1951	Italy	Belgium	Denmark	Italy	Belgium	Switzerland	Gr. Britain
1953	Czech.	U.S.S.R.	Yugoslavia	France	Denmark	Switzerland	U.S.S.R.
1954	U.S.S.R.	Denmark	Switzerland	Switzerland	Italy	Germany	U.S.S.R.
1955	Argentina	U.S.S.R.	Poland	Switzerland	Rumania	U.S.S.R.	U.S.S.R.
1956	Finland	U.S.S.R.	U.S.S.R.	Germany	Italy	U.S.S.R.	Czech.
1957	Germany	Gr. Britain	Australia	Gr. Britain	Germany	U.S.S.R.	Italy
1958	Germany	Finland	Australia	Germany	Germany	U.S.S.R.	Italy
1959	Germany	Germany	U.S.S.R.	Germany	Switzerland	U.S.S.R.	Germany
1961	Germany	Germany	U.S.S.R.	U.S.S.R.	Italy	U.S.S.R.	Italy
1962*	Germany	Germany	U.S.S.R.	Germany	Germany	France	Germany
1963	Germany	Italy	Czech.	Germany	Germany	Czech.	Germany
1964	U.S.S.R.	Holland	U.S.S.R.	Germany	Germany	U.S.S.R.	Germany
1965	U.S.S.R.	Denmark	Germany	U.S.S.R.	U.S.S.R.	Switzerland	Germany

*World Championships

Year–Place	Four with	Pair	Single	Pair with	Four without	Double	VIII	Quad
1966*	E. Ger.	E. Ger.	USA	Holland	E. Ger.	Switz	W. Ger.	
Bled	USSR	Aus.	Holland	France	USSR	USA	USSR	
	Yugoslavia	USSR	W. Ger.	Italy	Holland	E. Ger.	E. Ger.	
	Czech.	Poland	E. Ger.	E. Ger.	Hungary	Czech.	Gr. Brit.	
	Holland	W. Ger.	Denmark	USA	W. Ger.	Rumania	Yugoslavia	
	USA	Italy	USSR	W. Ger.	Denmark	W. Ger.	N. Zeal.	
1967	USSR	USA	E. Ger.	Italy	E. Ger.	Switz	W. Ger.	
Vichy	E. Ger.	E. Ger.	USSR	E. Ger.	Hungary	Bulgaria	USA	
	Roumania	W. Ger.	Holland	Czech.	USA	Czech.	USSR	
	Holland	Austria	W. Ger.	USSR	W. Ger.	USSR	E. Ger.	
	W. Ger.	Roumania	Denmark	W. Ger.	Roumania	Roumania	Holland	
	USA	USA	USA	Denmark	Switz	USA	Australia	
1968	N. Zeal	E. Ger.	Holland	Italy	E. Ger.	USSR	W. Ger.	
Mexico	E. Ger.	USA	W. Ger.	Holland	Hungary	Holland	Australia	
Olympics	Switz	Denmark	Argentina	Denmark	Italy	USA	USSR	
	Italy	Austria	USA	E. Ger.	Switz	Bulgaria	N. Zeal.	
	USA	Switz	E. Ger.	USA	USA	E. Ger.	Czech.	
	W. Ger.	Holland	Gr. Brit.	W. Ger.	W. Ger.	W. Ger.	USA	
1969	W. Ger.	USA	Argentina	Czech.	USSR	USA	E. Ger.	
Klagenfurt	E. Ger.	E. Ger.	E. Ger.	Italy	Hungary	Austria	USSR	
	Switz	Denmark	W. Ger.	Roumania	E. Ger.	E. Ger.	W. Ger.	
	Roumania	W. Ger.	Gr. Brit.	Switz.	Holland	W. Ger.	Holland	
	Holland	Poland	Czech.	USSR	W. Ger.	USSR	Gr. Brit.	
	USSR		Holland	E. Ger.	Italy	Switz.	Hungary	
1970*	W. Ger.	E. Ger.	Argentina	Roumania	E. Ger.	Denmark	E. Ger	
St.	E. Ger.	Poland	E. Ger.	E. Ger.	W. Ger.	E. Ger.	USSR	
Catherine's	Norway	W. Ger.	Czech.	USSR	Denmark	USA	N. Zeal.	
Canada	N. Zeal.	USSR	USSR	Italy	Holland	USSR	W. Ger.	
	Argentina	Switz.	W. Ger.	W. Ger.	Switz.	W. Ger.	Australia	
	USSR	Holland	Italy	Czech.	USSR	Switz	Poland	
1971	W. Ger.	E. Ger.	Argentina	E. Ger.	E. Ger.	E. Ger.	N. Zeal.	
	E. Ger.	Czech.	E. Ger.	Czech.	Norway	Norway	E. Ger.	
Copenhagen	USSR	Poland	N. Zeal.	USSR	W. Ger.	USSR	USSR	
	N. Zeal.	USSR	W. Ger.	Roumania	Roumania	Denmark	Hungary	
	Switz	Yugoslavia	USSR	Poland	USSR	Belgium	Holland	
	Czech.	Roumania	USA	Holland	Italy	Brazil	W. Ger.	
1972	W. Ger.	E. Ger.	USSR	E. Ger.	E. Ger.	USSR	N. Zeal.	
	E. Ger.	Swiss	Argentina	Czech.	N. Zeal.	Norway	USA	
Munich	Czech.	Holland	E. Ger.	Roumania	W. Ger.	E. Ger.	E. Ger.	
Olympics	USSR	Czech.	W. Ger.	W. Ger.	USSR	Denmark	USSR	
	USA	Poland	USA	USSR	Roumania	Gr. Brit.	W. Ger.	
	N. Zeal.	Roumania	Swiss	Poland	Denmark	Czech.	Poland	
1973	USSR	Roumania	W. Ger.	USSR	E. Ger.	E. Ger.	E. Ger.	
	E. Ger.	N. Zeal.	USSR	E. Ger.	USSR	USSR	Czech.	
Moscow	Czech.	W. Ger.	E. Ger.	Roumania	Norway	Gr. Brit.	USSR	
	USA	USSR	Argentina	France	W. Ger.	Czech.	Hungary	
	Norway	E. Ger.	Bulgaria	Czech.	Swiss	W. Ger.	W. Ger.	
	Bulgaria	Poland	Ireland	Poland	Roumania	Bulgaria	USA	
1974*	E. Ger.	E. Ger.	USA	USSR	E. Ger.	E. Ger.	USA	
	USSR	Norway	USA	E. Ger.	USSR	USSR	Gr. Brit.	
Lucerne	W. Ger.	Gr. Brit.	USSR	Czech.	W. Ger.	Czech.	N. Zeal.	
	Czech.	Czech.	Italy	Italy	N. Zeal.	Swiss	E. Ger.	
	Bulgaria	USSR	Argentina	France	USA	N. Zeal.	USSR	
	USA	Italy	Finland	Roumania	Norway	Bulgaria	W. Ger.	
1975*	USSR	E. Ger.	W. Ger.	E. Ger.	E. Ger.	Norway	E. Ger.	E. Ger.
	E. Ger.	Bulgaria	Ireland	Poland	USSR	E. Ger.	USSR	Czech.
Nottingham	W. Ger.	Holland	E. Ger.	W. Ger.	Roumania	Gr. Brit.	N. Zeal.	USSR
	Gr. Brit.	Finland	Finland	USSR	Gr. Brit.	Czech.	Czech.	France.
	Czech.	Poland	Argentina	USA	Czech.	W. Ger.	USA	Bulgaria
	Roumania	Roumania	USSR	Czech.	W. Ger.	USSR	Australia	Gr. Brit.

Year–Place	Four unit	Pair	Single	Pair with	Four without	Double	VIII	Quad
1976	USSR	E. Ger.	Finland	E. Ger.	E. Ger.	Norway	E. Ger.	W. Ger.
	E. Ger.	USA	W. Ger.	USSR	Norway	Gr. Brit.	Gr. Brit.	USSR
Montreal	W. Ger.	W. Ger.	E. Ger.	Czech.	USSR	E. Ger.	N. Zeal.	Czech.
Olympics	Czech.	Yugoslavia	Ireland	Poland	N. Zeal.	W. Ger.	W. Ger.	E. Ger.
	Bulgaria	Bulgaria	Argentina	Bulgaria	Canada	France	Australia	Bulgaria
	N. Zeal.	Czech.	USSR	Italy	W. Ger.	USSR	Czech.	USA
1977*	E. Ger.	USSR	E. Ger.	Bulgaria	E. Ger.	Gr. Brit.	E. Ger.	E. Ger.
	W. Ger.	Gr. Brit.	Finland	E. Ger.	N. Zeal.	E. Ger.	USSR	Czech.
Amsterdam	Bulgaria	E. Ger.	USSR	Czech.	Czech.	USSR	W. Ger.	Bulgaria
	USSR	Yugoslavia	Gr. Brit.	Holland	Holland	W. Ger.	Czech.	Spain
	Czech.	Bulgaria	Ireland	Roumania	Canada	USA	Gr. Brit.	France
	Yugoslavia	USA	Italy	Poland	Bulgaria	Czech.	USA	W. Ger.
1978*	E. Ger.	E. Ger.	W. Ger.	E. Ger.	USSR	Norway	E. Ger.	E. Ger
	W. Ger.	Gr. Brit.	E. Ger.	E. Ger.	E. Ger.	W. Ger.	W. Ger.	France
New Zealand	Bulgaria	France	Yugoslavia	Poland	Gr. Brit.	Switz	N. Zeal.	W. Ger.
	USA	Holland	USSR	W. Ger.	France	E. Ger.	Australia	Czech.
		Ireland	Argentina	Bulgaria	Czech.	USA	France	Bulgaria
		USA	Finland	Ireland	W. Ger.	N. Zeal.	Bulgaria	Spain
1979	E. Ger.	E. Ger.	Finland	E. Ger.	E. Ger.	Norway	E. Ger.	E. Ger.
Bled	USSR	USSR	W. Ger.	Czech.	Czech.	Czech.	N. Zeal.	W. Ger.
	W. Ger.	Swiss	E. Ger.	USA	Gr. Brit.	E. Ger.	USSR	France
	USA	Gr. Brit	Sweden	Yugoslavia	USSR	Gr. Brit.	Australia	Yugoslavia
	Spain	W. Ger.	Gr. Brit.	Roumania	Holland	Switz	USA	USA
	Bulgaria	Denmark	USSR	Bulgaria	Switz	W. Ger.	Gr. Brit.	Bulgaria

American Rowing and World Regattas, Women, 1964-1979

Modern rowing for women in this country had to found its own organization in 1964 (NWRA) to get started and only recently has become part of the NAAO. In Europe women's rowing also began on its own with little help from established boat clubs for men. The first European Championships for women were held in 1954 in Amsterdam and came under FISA auspices in 1962. American women first participated in the European Championships in 1967.

WOMEN'S ROWING—WORLD REGATTAS

	IV with	Singles	Quad with	Double	VIII	Pair	USA
1967 Vichy	E. Ger.	E. Ger.	USSR	USSR	USSR		
	USSR	Czech.	Hungary	E. Ger.	E. Ger.		
	Rumania	USSR	Bulgaria	Holland	Rumania		
	Hungary	Hungary	E. Ger.	W. Ger.	Holland	USA quad	
	Czech.	Holland	France	Rumania	Czech.	withdrew after	
	Denmark	Austria	Czech.		USA	first heat	
1969 Klagenfurt	USSR	USSR	USSR	E. Ger.	E. Ger.		
	E. Ger.	E. Ger.	Rumania	Czech.	USSR	USA single 10th	
	W. Ger.	Austria	W. Ger.	USSR	Rumania	USA VII 7th	
	Rumania	W. Ger.	Czech.	Bulgaria	Holland		
	Czech.	France	Bulgaria	Holland	Hungary		
	Hungary	Rumania	Hungary	Rumania	Czech.		
1970 Budapest	USSR	E. Ger.	Rumania	E. Ger.	E. Ger.		
	E. Ger.	Holland	USSR	USSR	USSR		
	W. Ger.	USSR	E. Ger.	Bulgaria	Rumania		USA Single
	Bulgaria	Austria	Bulgaria	France	Hungary		lost in
	Czech.	Poland	Czech.	Holland	Czech.		repechage
	Hungary	Denmark	W. Ger.	Czech.	Holland		
1971 Copenhagen	USSR	E. Ger.	Rumania	USSR	USSR		
	Rumania	France	USSR	E. Ger.	E. Ger.		USA Quad
	E. Ger.	W. Ger.	France	W. Ger.	Rumania		9th
	W. Ger.	Rumania	W. Ger.	France	Holland		USA
	Bulgaria	Denmark	Bulgaria	Poland	Hungary		Single 11th
	Holland	Holland	E. Ger.	Czech	Denmark		
1972 Brandenburg E. Ger.	USSR	Holland	Rumania	USSR	USSR	USA Single DNQ	
	E. Ger.	France	USSR	Holland	Rumania	USA Quad 8th	
	Holland	E. Ger.	W. Ger.	France	E. Ger.		
	France	W. Ger.	E. Ger.	W. Ger.	Hungary		
	Rumania	USSR	Czech.	Bulgaria	Holland		
	W. Ger.	Poland	France	E. Ger.	Czech.		
	Holland	USSR	E. Ger.	USSR	USSR	IV with: USA 9th	
	E. Ger.	Belgium	Rumania	Holland	E. Ger.	Quad USA 9th	
1973 Moscow	Poland	W. Ger.	USSR	W. Ger.	Rumania	Double USA 9th	
	USSR	Bulgaria	W. Ger.	Bulgaria	Hungary	VIII USA 7th	
	Bulgaria	E. Ger.	Czech.	Poland	Bulgaria		
	France	USA	Bulgaria	France	Poland		
1974 Lucerne	E. Ger.	E. Ger.	E. Ger.	USSR	E. Ger.	Rumania	Double last in series
	Holland	USSR	Rumania	W. Ger.	USSR	E. Ger.	Single 10
	Rumania	Belgium	USSR	E. Ger.	Rumania	USSR	Quad 8
							VIII lost in series

	IV with	Singles	Quad with	Double	VIII	Pair	USA
	France	W. Ger.	W. Ger.	Poland	W. Ger.	Czech.	
	USSR	France	Czech.	Holland	Holland	USA	
	Poland	Bulgaria	Hungary	Bulgaria	Poland	W. Ger.	
1975 Nottingham	E. Ger.	E. Ger.	E. Ger.	USSR	E. Ger.	E. Ger.	USA
	Bulgaria	Hungary	Bulgaria	E. Ger.	USA	USSR	Double 9
	W. Ger.	USSR	USSR	Bulgaria	Rumania	Rumania	Pair 8
	Holland	W. Ger.	Hungary	W. Ger.	W. Ger.	Bulgaria	
	USSR	USA	USA	Czech.	USSR	Poland	
	USA	Poland	Rumania	France	Hungary	Czech.	
1976 Montreal	E. Ger.	E. Ger.	E. Ger.	Bulgaria	E. Ger.	Bulgaria	USA
	Bulgaria	USA	USSR	E. Ger.	USSR	E. Ger.	
	USSR	USSR	Rumania	USSR	USA	W. Ger.	Quad 7
Olympics	Rumania	Bulgaria	Bulgaria	Norway	Canada	USSR	Pair 7
	Holland	Holland	Czech.	USA	W. Ger.	Canada	
	USA	Hungary	Denmark	Canada	Rumania	Rumania	
1977 Amsterdam	E. Ger.	E. Ger.	E. Ger.	Gr. Brit.	E. Ger.	E. Ger.	USA
	W. Ger.	Bulgaria	Czech.	E. Ger.	USSR	Holland	IV with 9
	Bulgaria	Hungary	Bulgaria	USSR	W. Ger.	Canada	Quad 8
	USSR	Russia	Spain	W. Ger.	Czech.	Rumania	
	Czech.	USA	France	USA	Gr. Brit.	Bulgaria	
	Jugoslavia	France	W. Ger.	Czech.	USA	USA	
1979 Bled	USSR	Rumania	E. Ger.	E. Ger.	USSR	E. Ger.	USA
	E. Ger.	E. Ger.	Bulgaria	Bulgaria	E. Ger.	Rumania	IV with 9
	Rumania	Holland	Rumania	Rumania	USA	Poland	
	Bulgaria	Canada	USSR	USSR	Rumania	Holland	
	Australia	USA	Hungary	USA	Canada	USA	
	W. Ger.	Bulgaria	USA	Poland	Bulgaria	Bulgaria	

American Rowing and the Olympics, 1900-1976

The ancient Olympic Games did not include any rowing events. But the founder of the modern Olympics, convinced that rowing was "the most complete sport that one could imagine," insisted on the inclusion of four rowing events in the second of the modern Games in 1900. Crews from nine nations participated, and such comparative newcomers as Germany, Holland and France showed their English teacher how well the lesson was learned. The American VIII from Vesper began a winning tradition. Some of the logistical problems of selecting, financing and transporting a rowing team to a distant international regatta were already enough to hold down the entries. The two world wars tragically interrupted the sequence in 1916, 1940 and 1944. But by 1976 rowers from 23 different countries competed at Montreal.

AMERICA AT THE OLYMPICS

	IV with	Pair without	Single	Pair with	IV without	Double	Eight
1900 Paris	Germany	Belgium	France	Holland	France		USA
	Neth.	Belgium	France	France	France		(Vesper)
	Germany	France	England	France	France		Belgium
							Neth.
1904 St. Louis		USA	USA		USA	USA	USA
		USA	USA		USA	USA	(Vesper)
		USA	USA		USA	USA	Canada
1908 Henley		Gr. Brit.	Gr. Brit.		Gr. Brit.		Gr. Brit.
		Gr. Brit.	Gr. Brit.		Gr. Brit.		Belgium
1912 Stockholm	Germany		Gr. Brit.				Gr. Brit.
1920 Antwerp	Switz.		USA	Italy	Gr. Brit.	USA	USA
	USA		(Kelly)	France		(Kelly-Costello)	(Navy)
	Norway		Gr. Brit.	Switz		France	Gr. Brit.
1924 Paris	Switz.		Gr. Brit.	Switz.	Gr. Brit.	USA	USA
	France		USA	Italy	Canada	(Kelly-Costello)	(Yale)
	USA		(Gilmore)	USA	Switz.	France	Canada
			Switz.			Switz.	Italy
1928 Amsterdam	Italy	Germany	Australia	Switz.	Gr. Brit.	USA	USA
	Switz.	Gr. Brit.	USA	France	USA	Canada	(California)
			(Myers)				Gr. Brit.
1932 Los Angeles	Germany	Gr. Brit.	Australia	USA	Gr. Brit.	USA	USA
	Italy	N. Zeal.	USA	Poland	Germany	Germany	(California)
	Poland	Poland	(Miller)	France	Italy	Canada	Italy
			Uruguay				Canada
1936 Berlin	Gremany	Germany	Germany	Germany	Germany	Gr. Brit.	USA
	Switz.	Denmark	Austria	Italy	Gr. Brit.	Germany	(Washington)
	France	Argentina	USA	France	Swiss	Poland	Italy
			(Burrows)				Germany
1948 Henley	USA	Gr. Brit.	Australia	Denmark	Italy	Gr. Brit.	USA
	Switz.	Switz.	Uruguay	Italy	Denmark	Denmark	(California)
	Denmark	Italy	Italy	Hungary	USA	Uruguay	Gr. Brit.
							Norway

	IV with	Pair without	Single	Pair with	IV without	Double	Eight
1952 Helsinki	Czech. Switz. USA	USA (Legg-Price) Belgium Switz.	USSR Australia Poland	France Germany Denmark	Yugoslavia France Finland	Argentina Russia Uruguay	USA (Navy) USSR Australia
1956 Melbourne	Italy Sweden Finland	USA USSR Austria	USSR Australia USA (Kelly)	USA Germany USSR	Canada USA France	Russia USA Australia	USA (Yale) Canada Australia
1960 Rome	Germany France Italy	USSR Austria Finland	USSR Germany Poland	Germany USSR USA	USA Italy USSR	Czech. Russia Switz.	Germany Canada Czech.
1964 Tokyo	Germany Italy Holland	Canada N. Zeal. Germany	USSR Germany Switz.	USA France N. Zeal.	Denmark Gr. Brit. USA	Russia USA (Storm-Cromwell) Czech.	USA (Vesper) Germany Czech.
1968 Mexico City	New Zeal. E. Ger. Switz.	E. Ger. USA (Hough Johnson) Denmark	Holland W. Ger. Argentina	Italy Holland Denmark	E. Ger. Hungary Italy	Russia Holland USA (Maher-Nunn)	W. Ger. Australia USSR
1972 Munich	W. Ger. E. Ger. Czech.	E. Ger. Switz. Holland	USSR Argentina E. Ger.	E. Ger. Czech. Roumania	E. Ger. N. Zeal. W. Ger.	USSR Norway E. Ger.	N. Zeal. USA E. Ger.
1976 Montreal	USSR E. Ger. W. Ger.	E. Ger. USA (Coffey, Staines) W. Ger.	Finland W. Ger. E. Ger.	E. Ger. USSR Czech.	E. Ger. Norway USSR	Norway Gr. Brit. E. Ger.	E. Ger. Gr. Brit. N. Zeal.

Quad

W. Ger.
Russia
Czech.

WOMEN'S OLYMPIC ROWING

	IV with	Doubles	Pair without	Single	Quad with	VIII
1976 Montreal	E. Ger. Bulgaria USSR	Bulgaria E. Ger. USSR	Bulgaria E. Ger. W. Ger.	E. Ger. USA (Lind) USSR	E. Ger. USSR Roumania	E. Ger. USSR USA

New England Scholastic
Rowing Association, 1948-1979

Schoolboy rowing in America began over a century ago, at first in the Eastern boarding schools whose graduates were sending back stories of the delights of boat racing. In 1871 the students at St. Paul's formed two boat clubs whose races provided the climax of the boating year. Twelve years later both the Harvard and Yale varsities were stroked by graduates of St. Paul's. (Harvard won by over a minute at four miles!) Most schools began rowing in IVs and continued to feature intramural or club racing. But match races eventually followed, with other schools or college lightweight VIIIs. Kent first journeyed to Henley in 1927; in 1929 Browne and Nichols won the Thames Cup. Finally in 1948 the New England Scholastic Championships were first held. Lake Quinsigamond at Worcester has proved a very central, satisfactory locale. The IVs race over three-quarters of a mile; the VIIIs, over a mile. Under the joint influence of the women's movement and the coming of coeducation to many of the schools, races for girls were added in 1974.

N.E.R.A. BOYS IVs

Year	First Boat	Second Boat	Third Boat	Fourth Boat
1948	Pomfret	Pomfret		
1949	Pomfret	Pomfret		
1950	Pomfret	Pomfret		
1951	Pomfret	Exeter		
1952	Exeter	Browne & Nichols		
1953	Browne & Nichols	Pomfret		
1954	Browne & Nichols	Browne & Nichols		
1955	Gunnery	Gunnery		
1956	Gunnery	Pomfret	Exeter	
1957	Pomfret	Exeter	Browne & Nichols	
1958	Pomfret	Exeter	Exeter	
1959	Bel. Hill/B & N	Exeter	Exeter	
1960	Exeter	Exeter	Exeter	
1961	So. Kent	Bel. Hill/Exeter	Exeter	
1962	Exeter	Exeter	Exeter	
1963	Brooks	Groton	Noble & Greenough	
1964	Groton	Groton	Exeter	
1965	Exeter	So. Kent	Exeter	
1966	So. Kent	So. Kent	Noble & Greenough	
1967	Brooks	So. Kent	Noble & Greenough	
1968	Noble & Greenough	Pomfret	Exeter	

Year	First Boat	Second Boat	Third Boat	Fourth Boat
1969	Noble & Greenough	Belmont Hill	Belmont Hill	
1970	Noble & Greenough	Belmont Hill	Belmont Hill	
1971	Belmont Hill	So. Kent	So. Kent	
1972	Brooks	So. Kent	So. Kent	
1973	So. Kent	Belmont Hill	Brooks	Belmont Hill
1974	Browne & Nichols	Brooks	Brooks	Belmont Hill
1975	Saint Marks	Saint Marks	Belmont Hill	Belmont Hill
1976	Belmont Hill	Belmont Hill	Browne & Nichols	Brooks
1977	Brooks	Browne & Nichols	Saint Marks	Groton
1978	Salisbury	Brooks	Brooks	Belmont Hill
1979	Groton	Groton	Middlesex	Salisbury

N.E.I.R.A. BOYS VIIIs

Year	First Boat	Second Boat	Third Boat
1951	Kent	Browne & Nichols	
1952	Tabor	Kent	
1953	Kent	Kent	
1954	Shrewsbury	Halcyon	
1955	Shattuck	Shattuck	
1956	Kent	Andover	
1957	Kent	Kent	
1958	Kent	Kent	
1959	Andover	Kent	
1960	Kent	Kent	
1961	Kent	Kent	
1962	Andover	Kent	
1963	Kent	Kent	
1964	Andover	Andover	
1965	Andover	Kent	
1966	Halcyon	Kent	
1967	Kent	Kent	
1968	Kent	Kent	
1969	Kent	Andover	
1970	Kent	St. Pauls	
1971	Northfield-Mt. Hermon	Exeter	
1972	Kent	Exeter	
1973	Exeter	Exeter	Exeter
1974	St. Paul's	St. Paul's	St. Paul's
1975	St. Paul's	Exeter	Exeter
1976	St. Paul's	Tabor	Exeter
1978	Kent	St. Paul's	St. Paul's
1979	St. Paul's	St. Paul's	St. Paul's
1980	Exeter	Kent	Exeter

N.E.I.R.A. BOYS SINGLES

Year	Senior	Junior
1961	Choate	
1962	Pomfret	
1963	Choate	
1964	Choate	
1965	So. Kent	
1966	Choate	
1967	Choate	
1968	Choate	
1969	St. John's	
1970	Belmont Hill	
1971	Choate	
1972	So. Kent	
1973	Choate	
1974	Moses Brown	Choate
1975	Moses Brown	Choate
1976	Barrington	Barrington
1977		
1978	Andover	Moses Brown
1979	East Lyme	So. Kent

NEIRA: GIRLS

	IVs			VIIIs			Singles
Year	First Boat	Second Boat	Third Boat	First Boat	Second Boat	Third Boat	
1974				St. Paul's			
1975	So. Kent	Nobles & Green		St. Paul's	Northfield Mt. H.		
1976	Pomfret	Middlesex		St. Paul's	St. Paul's		
1977	Middlesex	Middlesex	Nobles & Green	Andover	St. Paul's	Simsbury	
1978	Middlesex	Groton	Middlesex	St. Paul's	St. Paul's	Simsbury	
1979	Groton	Groton	Groton	St. Paul's	St. Paul's	St. Paul's	East Lyme